Taken from the author's film strip, Characterization and Stage Positions, *this picture shows a group in Hebrew costumes. The women are wearing New Testament apparel, the men either New or Old Testament clothing.*

Biblical Costumes

for CHURCH and SCHOOL

by Virginia Wilk Elicker

illustrated by Elva Droz Hamilton

A. S. Barnes and Company New York

Manufactured in the United States of America.

Published on the same day in the Dominion of Canada by The Copp Clark Company, Ltd., Toronto.

Library of Congress Catalog Card Number: 53-8301

To Lyman

Preface

In writing a book of this kind, many influences play important roles. The most important is experience.

After mastering the principles of production, comes the adapting of those principles to the special occasion, with no two occasions being alike. One group can afford to buy a limited amount of material, another group can not even call upon the members of the cast to supply the wherewithal for individual costumes, while still another has no idea what to do with what it has.

Ingenuity, then, is needed. What can be substituted for the real article and still give the appearance of the article in demand? Over a period of years, the amassing of ideas, not only from the field of dramatics, but from many other phases of life, has given the author ample opportunity to sift through all the ideas, discard those that have been found wanting, and to retain the rest that they may be further refined.

The adaptation of the historic Biblical costume to meet the needs of the individual group has been fun. There is a definite thrill which arises from creating, from practically nothing, a well-costumed character that the average audience easily recognizes and delights in seeing.

The Euclid Avenue Baptist Church in Cleveland, Ohio, for eighteen years provided the author with many an opportunity to prove the efficacy of more than one costume. That church has the author's deep appreciation for providing not only a testing ground, but also an opportunity to demonstrate the well-founded principles of good theater.

The schools and many small churches with which the author has either worked or had contact have opened avenues of research. The author is grateful for their problems, and hopes this volume will help others who have found it difficult to costume a character effectively, having either scant knowledge or little material with which to work.

Introduction

Many audiences of Biblical dramatic productions have preconceived ideas as to how a character should appear. To many come to mind pictures of the Hebrew in flowing robes, of an image in beard and bare feet, or of the cheesecloth-draped child in a Sunday school production of the Nativity scene. Others may even remember from pictures of the masters the robes of the Middle Ages. In planning costumes for the Biblical play, it is important to consider not only the authentic dress of the times, but also what the audience will accept as familiar.

Of course, all are aware of the fact that peoples other than the Hebrews walked the pages of Biblical history. Among these others were the Egyptians, Assyrians, Persians, Greeks and Romans—all of whom influenced not only the dress of the Hebrews but also of each other.

A number of excellent books describe the authentic garb of the different nations that waxed and waned in Biblical times. With only minor differences, these books are in agreement in depicting these ancient peoples and how they influenced the dress of those they conquered or those who mingled willingly with them. No sharp line of demarkation may be drawn between the different periods of civilization. The periods continually overlapped, and basic styles as well as accessories were carried back and forth from country to country and tribe to tribe. For instance, the early Babylonian costume was carried into the Assyrian period, which was subsequently absorbed into the later Babylonian, and we have what is called the Assyrian-Babylonian period. The stories of Abraham, Moses and Joseph join the Chaldean and Hebrew to the Egyptian era.

However historically accurate one desires the portrayal of a Biblical story to be, the audience and the dramatic quality of the scene must always be kept in mind. To place before an audience a group of characters in costumes peculiar and unfamiliar is to call undue attention to the wearing apparel instead of to the story and characters. Unintentional humor is likely to creep into a scene. Characters wearing costumes which may be authentic but which are in contrast to the already-formed mental images of the members of the audience, or are reminiscent of a common article of modern wearing apparel, tend to overemphasize the seeming incongruity of the picture. Instances of this would be the cheese-box headdress that Abraham might have worn as a prince in the Chaldees, or the pointed turban that reminds one of an old-fashioned nightcap, both of which could easily evoke laughter rather than induce a feeling of reverence. Care must be taken to anticipate audience reaction, especially in regard to laughter that is out of place. The mental images of audiences should be modified gradually. Good education is almost always a slow process, particularly in regard to religion, and drama used to teach religion should not startle the audience. Shock in religious drama, to the audience eye and ear, is either offensive or humorous. Offensiveness should never exist and only when it is intended should humor get a reaction from the audience. It is good to be authentic but strict authenticity is not always wise, especially in respect to religious drama given by amateur groups.

Hence the necessity of dressing the characters not only in garments that will be acceptable either to church or school audiences, but also in keeping with the country in which these characters lived or by which their dress was influenced. This can be done by giving a general indication of a certain characteristic of time or period but tempering the harsh lines, thereby achieving an over-all indefiniteness. This is much to be preferred to a close "sticking-to-the-book." Unless the dramatization is for educational purposes rather than inspirational message, it is better that the costumes be indefinite than attempt to be authentic and fail in two or more details.

In this book we shall try to present some historical background for the dress of the more prominent Biblical characters and then offer suggestions as to how these characters may be clothed—keeping in mind the salient features that emphasize the outstanding differences of dress. There are certain basic garments that may be used, and a few changes made in these will alter their appearance considerably.

These suggestions are offered from much experience with small, amateur groups whose only qualification is a keen desire to portray something dramatic. Literally, this desire is all they have. There is little or no treasury for the luxury of a drama presentation. Hence, what costumes and accessories may be used that will be inexpensive but still be effective to project the desired message?

The preacher, the principal and the audience expect the utmost although they may not say so in as many words. They say, "Just something simple." But they do not want that "something simple" to *look* simple. So the teacher or person in charge does the best he can. Too frequently, however, the results have all the earmarks of hastily gathered old bathrobes, shawls, scarves and whatever else is available.

Time, also, is usually important—no time to make the simplest of costumes because the decision to have a Christmas play was late. It is odd that church organizations never seem to learn that whatever is presented in dramatic form *must* have plenty of time for preparation. A women's group may plan its season well in advance, but decide on the Nativity scene at its Christmas party so late that it is "Hurry and call Mrs. Morgan for the outfit she wore two years ago," or, "See if Mrs. Wilson has something that can be used." This happens more times than the author would care to enumerate. The large churches in the big cities are as much at fault as the smaller ones in the low-population communities when it comes to "putting on" dramatic presentations at the last moment.

Plenty of time is very essential to the assembling of costumes, and if some have to be made, even more time is required. If helpers need training, time should be allowed for that. Costuming a drama presentation is not an easy task if the right effect is desired.

The task, however, need not become a chore. Interesting results may be obtained with some background knowledge of basic garments and variations in them. Successful costumers have basic foundations which they change for the period and character by the addition of a ruffle here, the removal of a flounce there, or a different type of cuff—always keeping the foundation the same. Little tricks of the trade are very helpful in cutting corners, making the task a little easier and gaining pleasure from what could be a thankless and uninteresting job.

It is the purpose of this textbook to offer these little tricks to the person who needs ideas and techniques for costuming a Biblical presentation when the budget is low and workers are few and inexperienced.

V.W.E.

Contents

Section One

Basic Garments

The first consideration in costuming a Biblical play should be the selection of some basic garments which may be used with certain variations or with other additional parts of dress, thereby changing their appearance for the different characters and situations. There is one time-tested rule in regard to the handling of costumes for the stage: the initial cut of any costume should be simple, so that to the costume may be added items pertaining to the period in which the play takes place. These items—trimmings such as stripes, fringes, collars, embroidery on borders, and so forth—are usually sewn on in large but secure stitches, so that they may be removed easily. For stage use, a garment is never altered by cutting in order to fit a smaller person. Tucks, inverted pleats and turned-up hems are employed for the purpose of making costumes smaller. In this way a single garment will serve many purposes.

There are a number of references made to the use of cardboard in the making of both costumes and accessories. Most of these references pertain to the kind of cardboard that is fairly flexible, or in other words, cardboard of suit-box grade. At the present writing this is not difficult to obtain. Before cutting the pattern, the cardboard should be tested for the greatest flexibility. For instance, if the top of a suit-box is used, it should be bent first the long way and then the short way. It should bend without cracking. Whichever way it *bends* is the desirable way for making many articles that require stiff, curved surfaces.

Cheesecloth and tobacco cloth are suggested many times, not so much for foundations or tunics but for the many overdrapes and shawls that the different peoples adapted in various arrangements to their particular types of dress. Flannelette, unbleached muslin, and old sheets are inexpensive materials that may be made into attractive undergarments. In purchasing tobacco cloth and flannelette, we suggest you contact the South Carolina Mills, Spartanburg, South Carolina, where a good grade of these materials may be obtained in various colors and at reasonable cost.

The Undergarment

The undergarment, which was worn next to the body, was called the *chiton* by the Greeks, and *tunica* or *stola* by the Romans. In this text, this article of apparel will be referred to as the tunic or undergarment.

This undergarment may be made either from flannel, flannelette, heavy cotton or a sheet draped in a special manner. The following figures will illustrate both the sewed garment and the draping of a sheet.

For groups that are able to purchase materials, the tunic is easily made and serves on many occasions and for many characters. The garment consists of a straight piece of goods from shoulder to instep. The neck is open enough to slip over the head. There are armholes with no sleeves. This style is similar to the "princess slips" of some years ago. It is not very full and hangs straight, its adaptation being made to the women rather than the men. Figure 1A shows this type of tunic.

Figure 1B is similar to 1A except that it is fuller and has sewn-in sleeves of straight material. These sleeves may reach the elbow or wrist. When sewing in the sleeves, fairly large stitches should be used so that the sleeves may be removed easily. Smaller sleeves, as in Figure 1C, that just fit the arm may be basted in for certain characters after sewing up the larger armhole to fit the smaller sleeve. These smaller sleeves may also be sewn or fastened with snaps into the armholes of the tunic in Figure 1A. A foundation similar to Figure 1B or 1C may be worn by either men or women, Figure 1B being more appropriate for men of New Testament times, when the overdrape is used on the stage instead of the cloak.

These undergarments may be dyed any of the pastel shades. The cotton dyes are suitable, especially if flannelette is the material. Since the basic garments will be

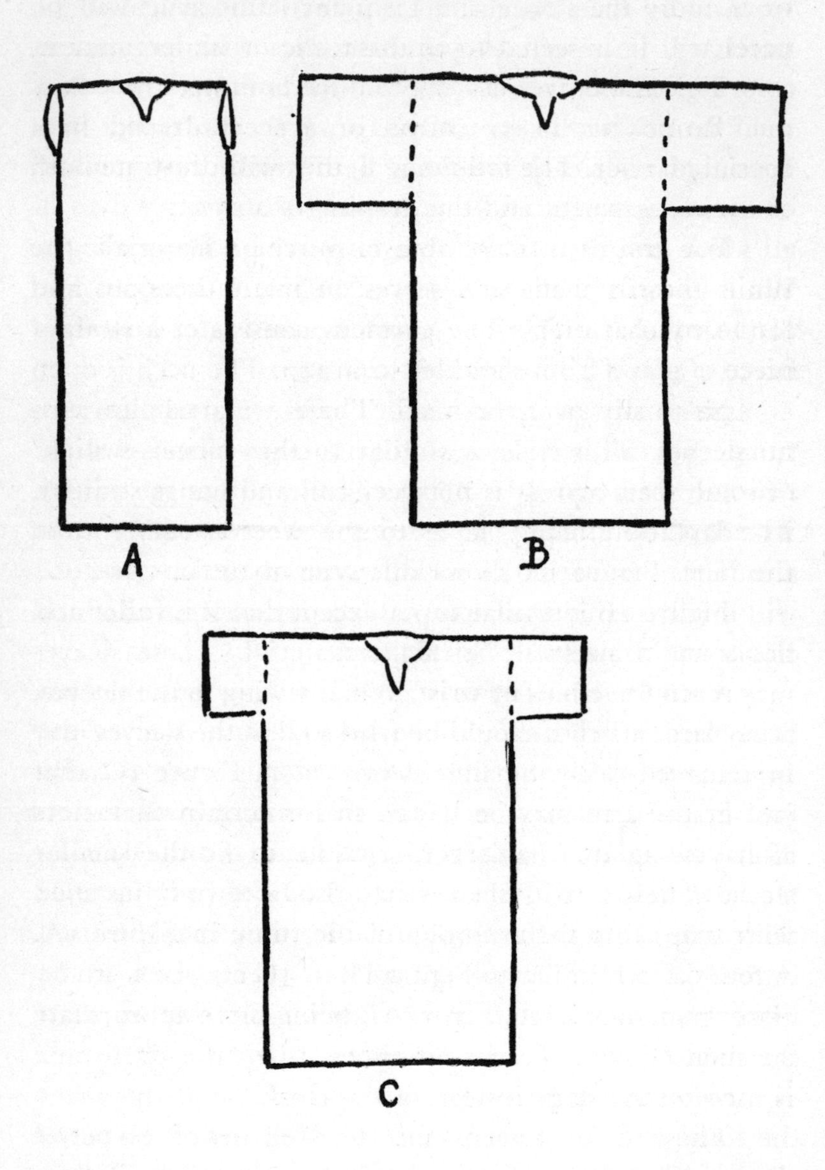

Figure 1—The sewed tunic.

worn more than once and frequent laundering will be necessary, it is well to purchase dyes with permanent coloring. These dyes usually require boiling. The colors then do not wash out easily. However, the tunics may be tinted after each washing, if the temporary method of dyeing is preferred. The ten-cent stores carry dyes of all kinds and directions for dyeing are on the packages. While the pastel shades may not be the authentic colors of the country or period, it will be seen later how they may be adapted for different characters.

Not many groups can afford to buy material for costumes but all have access to single-size sheets which, when draped correctly, make efficient tunics for adults. The first few attempts at draping a sheet usually end in a ludicrous imitation of a Halloween ghost, but practice will finally turn out an acceptable foundation over which cloaks and drapes will be effective.

A single sheet of fairly poor grade, or one that has been used many times, is the best because it gives the appearance of having been worn and falls more easily into graceful folds. A new sheet or one of good material has a tendency to keep its own identity and, no matter how well it is draped, still looks like bed linen. If there are colored sheets obtainable, they may be used instead of white. However, colored sheets seem to be more readily available in the double size rather than the single.

Following Figures 2A, 2B and 2C, take the sheet the long way and start at the front, throwing corner *a* over one shoulder. Here it is the left shoulder. Corner *b* should just touch the floor. If the person is short in

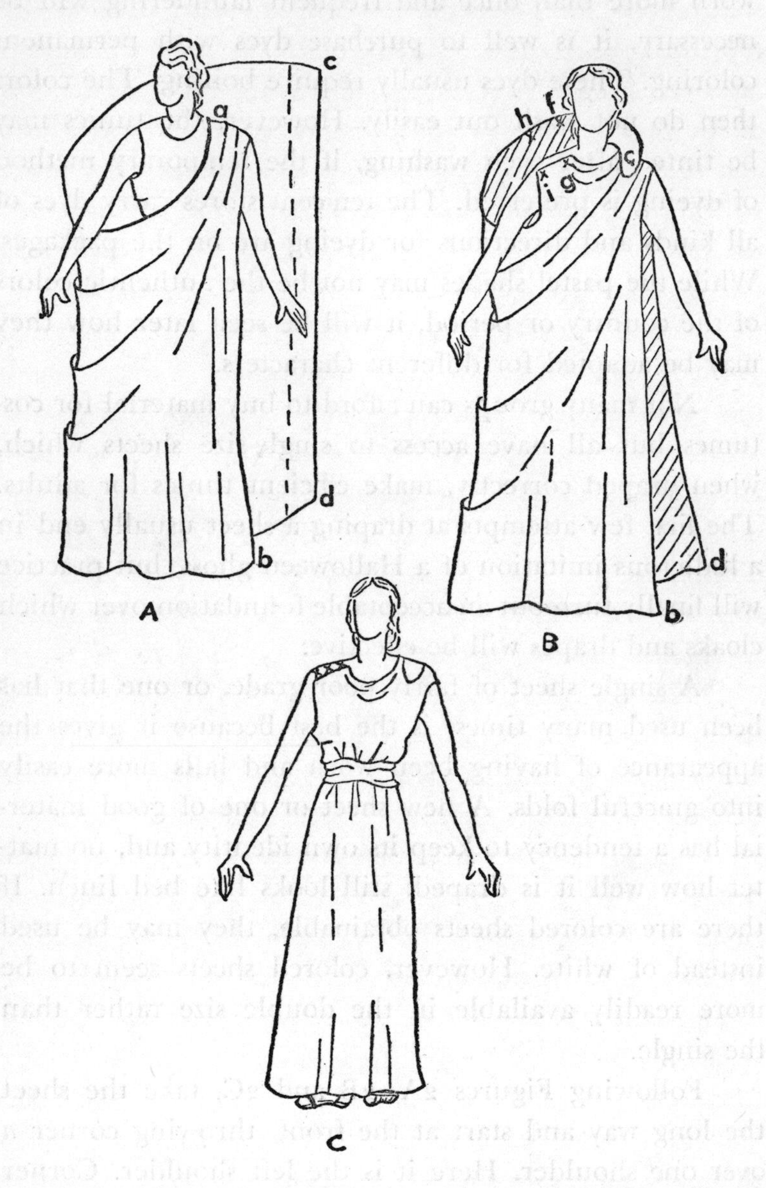

Figure 2—Draping of a sheet for use as a tunic.

stature, the sheet may be too long, so turn it *in* at the *top* until the right length is obtained. Corner *c* should lap over *a* as in Figure 2B. Then pull taut the section at the nape of the neck so that the distance between *f* and *c* in Figure 2B is only about five inches. Any more will allow the tunic to slip down over one shoulder or the other. Pin *underneath, g* to *f* and *i* to *h*. An extra pin may be needed to help form the right sleeve. Let the arms be raised shoulder-high while putting on the girdle so that there will be freedom of movement in the arms later. After the girdle is placed, adjust the open side so that the front laps over the back. Remove any "dips" below the girdle by giving slight tugs to the material above. The lines should be straight up and down and not like the scallops on a pantry shelf. Be sure the hem is straight, especially on the open side where the lapping occurs.

Thin, cotton blankets of plain color make excellent tunics for the men. However, a blanket for a double bed is often needed to cover a large male character. The blanket should be plain, no checks or borders.

The long tunics or foundations should not cover the feet. While some authentic pictures show the foundations gracefully falling in soft folds about the feet, it must be kept in mind that the characters in a play, although they might have but restricted action on the stage, have to make entrances and exits. It is so easy for modern casts, unaccustomed to flowing robes, to trip and not only tear the costume, but also cause injury to themselves. So care should be taken to keep the costume not any longer than just below the ankle.

Of course, if a character is discovered, that is, on the stage before the curtains are parted, and remains in one place as a statue on a pedestal until after the curtains are closed, and overlength folds are desired for artistic effect, the character may then wear them longer.

Egyptian

For basic Egyptian undergarments, see Section II, "The Time of Joseph," and "The Time of Moses," where specific characters are discussed.

Assyrian

In considering the Assyrian undergarment, it should be remembered that the Phoenicians, Philistines and some of the smaller tribes were greatly influenced by Assyria, a strong country that leaned decidedly toward the military. Therefore this tunic will not be used by Assyrian characters alone.

The undergarment for these people may be adapted from the small-sleeved or sleeveless tunic shown in Figures 1A and 1C. Fringe may be added to the bottom if desired. It was very often worn, and this addition will change the appearance of the tunic considerably.

The foundation for the women was like the long, small-sleeved tunic in the Figure 1C. Ordinarily the sleeves for the women were three-quarter length, but this is not necessary if the character wears plenty of bracelets, on the upper arm as well as the forearm. The

Assyrians were noted for the lavishness of their ornaments, both on their dress and on their bodies.

The length of the tunic for the men varied from the knee to the ankle, depending, not especially upon the rank, but the activity of the wearer. Hunters and horsemen wore their fringed tunics about to the calf of the leg and cut in front in the shape of an inverted "V." Obviously this allowed greater freedom both on and off a horse. If this type of garment is desired, use one of the fuller tunics, as Figure 1B, with the sleeves removed. Cut from top to bottom in the middle of the front and sew the cut edges together from the top to a little above the knee. Turn up the material at the bottom to the required length and baste a hem. Turn back the two corners at the bottom of the cut to form an inverted "V." Slightly round the angles at the bottom by turning back and taking small darts in the material. Since fringe was usually an important part of the early garments, especially of the Assyrian, baste a fringe on the outside of the hem, rounding the point of the inverted "V" as much as possible.

It is not a too neat-looking garment on the wrong side, but outside appearance is what is important, as is expediency. Any undue bunchiness will be alleviated after the garment is pressed. While the wisdom of cutting the tunic from top to bottom may seem doubtful, when a production with the Assyrian hunter is finished, his foundation may be restored to the realm of basic garments by taking off the fringe, letting down the hem and sewing together the section down the front. In our smaller auditoriums, where details are easily observed, a seam only halfway up looks like an accident, while a seam from top to bottom has the appearance of being there on purpose.

Grecian

There may be little use for the Greek dress in plays of Biblical times, but it should be described at some length because it influenced the Roman dress, and both Greek and Roman influenced the Hebrew of the New Testament. Besides, it is well to be familiar with the Greek dress because it is used frequently when classic figures are represented. Then, too, Paul's journeys took him to Greece, and one might want to dramatize some of his missionary experiences. Mary Magdalene was a Grecian woman and her costume would follow the Greek lines.

There are two types of Greek dress, the Doric and the Ionic, that shall be discussed here, either of which may be used in depicting characters in ancient Greece. Both employed the *chiton* (kī′tŏn), which was the tunic or foundation. The Doric chiton for women may be formed in the following manner.

Since the chiton was a rectangular piece of cloth, a sheet may be used for this garment. A double sheet will be needed for a person of average height, because it is draped differently from the undergarment described earlier. Taking the sheet the long way, fold over an eight-inch section on the *outside,* or enough so that the remaining width reaches from the shoulder to about two inches on the floor. Then double the material so that the center of the length is on the left side. The ends, which will form an open side, will be on the right as in Figure 3A. The body is between the folds.

Catch up the edge of the folded top in back at the shoulders and secure with pins to the edge of the front fold. This time the pins are not safety pins but should imitate the straight ones which were used in the Doric dress. Three-inch hat pins are suggested. When employed in ancient times, these pins attained such lengths that they could be used as weapons. An instance when this was true is spoken of by Herodotus (468 B.C.), who tells of the anguish and passion of the women who stabbed to death the only man to return from an unsuccessful battle, using their long pins as the instruments of death. Thereafter, they were forbidden to wear pins and the type of Ionic chiton was adopted which used no pins.

If these straight pins *are* used, in order to keep the points from becoming hazards, there should be guards on the tips. These guards may be found on the pins used as ornaments on women's hats. However, as most audiences are unaware of the fact that the ancients wore pins, even safety pins or *fibula* (fĭb′ū-lå) to hold together parts of the dress, it might be well to pin the sections mentioned so that they have the appearance of being sewed, which indeed was the case in many instances.

The Ionic chiton was formed in the same manner except that the material on the shoulders was either sewn together or buttons used where the pins had pre-

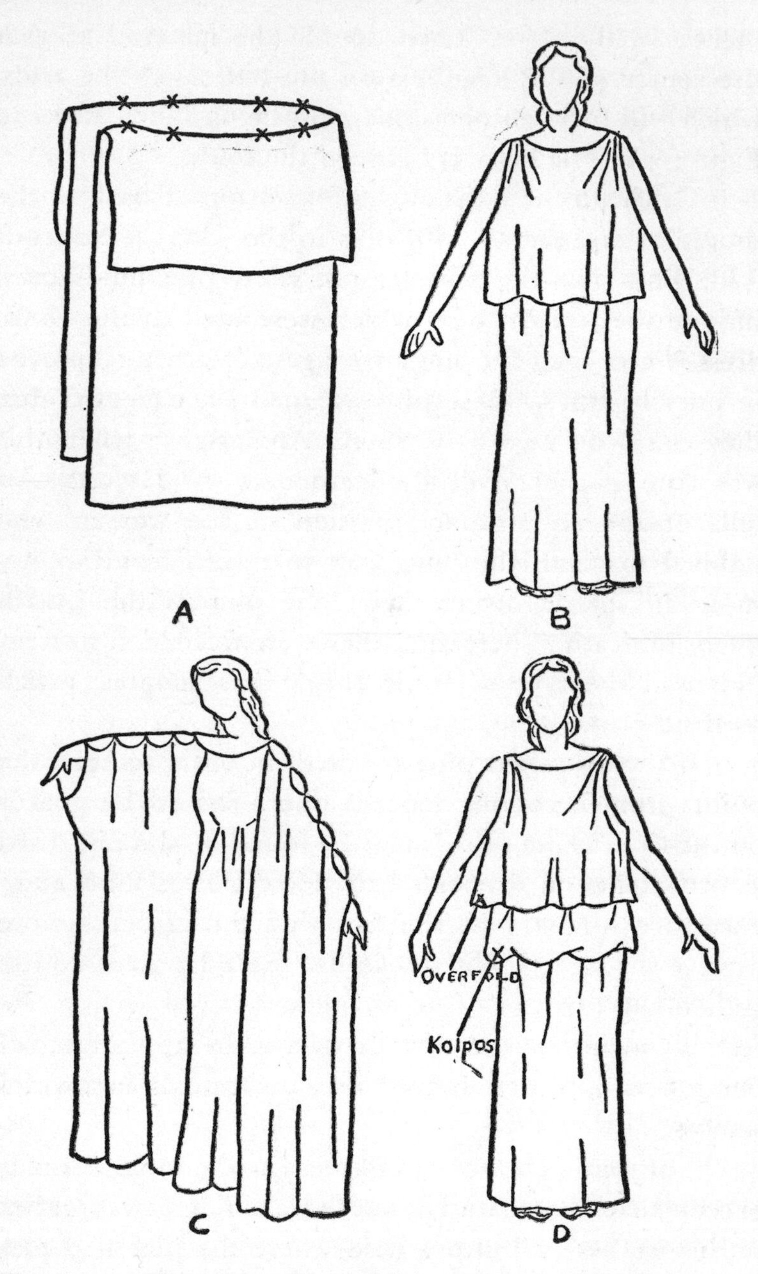

Figure 3—The sheet draped for a Greek chiton.

viously been. The remaining width of the front and back was caught together at one-inch intervals down the arms, sometimes with buttons, sometimes sewn, thus forming a sleeve of sorts with the last loop making the armhole, as in Figure 3C. Placing the girdle as described on page 60 formed a draped sleeve as shown in Figure 13C. This sleeve differentiated the Ionic chiton from the Doric, which just fastened on the shoulder. According to some authorities, the Ionic used finer material than the Doric and the folds were more delicate, but since the Ionic chiton seldom had the overfold, the draped sheet will not be too voluminous and bulky. However, if finer material is desired to simulate the delicate material of the Ionic chiton, two lengths of the Hebrew overdrape (see page 36) may be basted together with small stitches to form the chiton. Because of the transparency of the cheesecloth or tobacco cloth, a long nightgown or evening slip should be worn under this.

Under the overfold of the Doric chiton place a girdle around the natural waistline, and pull up over the girdle the surplus material which is on the floor. This will form a pouch or *kolpos* (kŏl′pŏs). The edge of the overfold often was bordered with intricate or simple designs. Figure 3D illustrates the different parts of the Doric chiton.

If the kolpos was allowed to reach a few inches below the hips, it was secured by a second girdle around the hips. This then formed what was known as the "peplos of Athena." Should this type of costume be desired, a double sheet is certainly needed. As was stated earlier in this section, the sheets used for foundations or tunics should be quite flimsy in texture, especially in the Greek chiton, so that the soft folds will more easily simulate the fine linen or woven flax worn by the ancient Greeks.

In regard to the men, the chiton was not differentiated as being Doric or Ionic. The undergarment was worn either to the knees or to the ankles, depending upon the amount of activity of the wearer. It was cut and sewn and had sleeves. However, if the chiton is to reach the ankles, a sheet may be draped in the same manner as that for the Doric woman.

Roman

The undergarment was called the *tunica* by the Romans. One of the fuller short-sleeved tunics, white if possible, may be used for male characters.

A Roman matron was known to wear several tunics at one time. These consisted of the *tunica interior* which was worn next to the body, the *stola* over that, with a special *stola* on the outside. The special *stola* was shorter hem. It was considered a mark of honor. The luxuriant and had a gold border, *patagium* (på-tā'jĭ-ŭm), on the Roman life advocated the use of many tunics, one worn over the other and of various colors.

For the amateur stage, all these tunics are not needed. The undertunic might easily be the draped sheet, the two pieces of Hebrew overdrape basted the long way together, or the tunic of Figure 1A. If either sheet or overdrape is used, it should be arranged in Ionic style with a girdle placed as described on page 60. Over this tunic, a shorter tunic open at the sides should be worn. This may be made of tobacco cloth dyed a deep blue and bordered with gold, and should reach either to the knees or a few inches below. A second girdle about the waist is placed over both tunics. If the undertunic had sleeves, the shorter tunic did not, and vice versa. So if the draped sheet is used, the shorter tunic should be sleeveless.

Another type of undertunic had long, close-fitting sleeves. If these are desired, the sleeves may be inserted with snaps into the sleeveless tunic, thus transforming the basic undergarment into a Roman *tunica*. This kind of costume with the long sleeves is especially good for Roman women of higher birth.

The Cloak and the Overdrape

Almost all ancient people wore some kind of cloak or overdrape. Sometimes these overgarments were worn for style, sometimes for protection against the elements, often according to the rank of the wearer or the amount of activity in which he was normally engaged. Two kinds of cloaks may be made, using the same type of material as the sewn undergarment or tunic.

The first one is cut along lines similar to the sleeveless undergarment except that it is open down the front and very much wider. (See Figure 4A.) It usually reached from fingertip to fingertip. However, hands are used for gestures on the stage, so it is better if the cloak extends only to the wrists. The cloak will trail on the ground when the arms are down at the sides, so that a

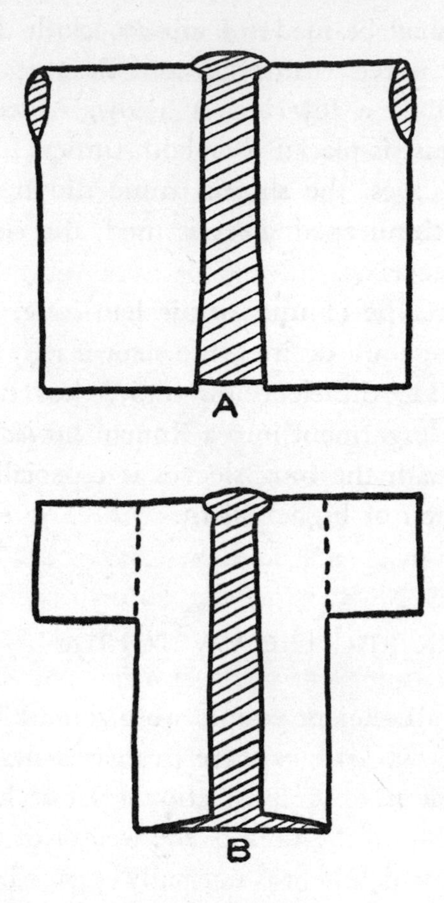

Figure 4—The cloak or Hebrew aba.

character who raises his arms for dramatic effect should have much practice in learning to keep his feet from becoming involved in the folds. Dress rehearsal is too late to begin practicing.

While this cloak takes much material and is very effective, the second type, with sewn-in sleeves, such as in Figure 4B, also gives a voluminous effect and probably is more adaptable. It is cut along the same lines as that of the sleeved tunic except that it contains more material and larger sleeves. Again the sleeves are sewn in with large stitches.

These cloaks may be made to look like very heavy material if flannelette is used. Dye the material dark brown, dark gray, wine red or dark yellow. While the material is still wet, brush it the wrong way so that the nap is raised. When dry, the material is rich-looking, sometimes taking on the appearance of velvet. Burlap sacks make excellent homespun cloaks. Ripped apart and sewn together, they are inexpensive enough to use for the sleeveless type which requires much material. Bleach the burlap first and then dye it any of the somber shades of brown, green, gray, ochre-yellow or wine red. On the wrong side around the neck, sew a yoke of soft material to protect the neck from the scratchy tendency of the burlap. Potato sacks are usually available, but care should be taken that whatever sacks are used are of the same weave and heft, the softer kind making better folds.

Hebrew

The *aba,* as the cloak was called by the Hebrews, was striped or plain, but use of wide stripes was typically Hebrew. Sometimes alternating colors were used, or a narrow stripe alternated with a wide, or a wide with a group of narrow. These stripes were varied in their use so different effects may be achieved by basting them on the abas. By omitting the stripes, the aba is still further transformed.

The aba was sometimes as wide as nine feet. Most of them were made of sheep's or camel's hair and were very heavy. This was an exceedingly useful garment because it could be made into a small tent for shelter at night when traveling, or the wearer could wrap it around him as he lay down to sleep. In fact, the cloak was such an important part of a man's possessions that it was punishable by law for anyone to take it from another.

The overdrapes, shawls and veils that were worn by many of the ancients, especially the women, may be made of either cheesecloth or tobacco cloth of good grade. Different lengths, ranging from three to four and one-half yards of white cloth may be dyed the pastel shades of blue, green, yellow, orange and orchid. Also, the darker shades—navy blue, dark green, dark yellow, purple and wine red. These lengths will be used in different ways as described later.

The shawl should be four yards long and one yard wide if made of cheesecloth. If tobacco cloth is used, it quite frequently is forty-three inches wide, which makes a better appearance for any use. Many of the shawls of the early peoples were fringed on all four sides. To keep the shawl a basic garment, the fringe may be made detachable, as in the following manner. Tear four-inch strips from an old cotton sheet; there should be enough to go around four sides of the shawl. Turn in one long edge of the strips and sew a narrow sturdy hem on a machine. Prepare the fringe by tearing the sheet strips into tiny sections, almost, but not quite, to the hem line. Dye the prepared fringe any dark color, or the same color as that of the shawl, and baste on the shawl. The fringe may thus be taken off so that the shawl may be used in some other capacity in another production. Quite often it is feasible to baste on the fringe in four pieces, the sections ending at the corners. In this way, the fringe on the sides of the two lengths may be removed, should fringe be desired only on the ends.

When these drapes are used in single thickness, especially with the pastel shades, a veil-like quality is achieved. For a heavier appearance resembling a velour use a double-thickness of the darker shades.

Assyrian

Often the Assyrians wore the tunic without a shawl, sometimes the shawl alone or, yet again, both together. For the purpose of the amateur stage it might be well to combine the tunic and the shawl. To make this particular shawl, sew together lengthwise two of the colored cheesecloth overdrapes and attach fringe to the two long sides. Fold back twenty-eight inches of the material, and at one end of the fold attach a five- or six-inch cord, as in Figure 5. Fasten this cord at the right side to a cord wound around the waist, and throw the shawl over the right shoulder toward the back. Bring the folded edge around the back of the neck and over the left shoulder to the front. Form a sling for the left arm by tucking the material in the waist cord. Tuck the folded edge up and over the waist cord, which will hold the

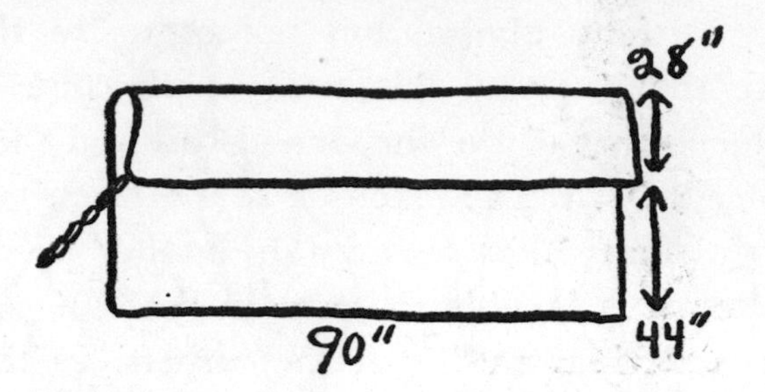

Figure 5—Pattern for Assyrian shawl.

shawl in place. Continue the edge around the back of the waist to the front, and whatever surplus there is, tuck under the cord at the left side and allow it to drape to the hemline of the tunic. With this type of draping, a diagonal fringe across the front is formed halfway to the waist, as well as one which almost reaches the hem of the tunic. See Figure 6A. An Assyrian king might wear this kind of dress.

A simpler method of draping the king is to use double thicknesses of tobacco cloth, fringed on the two long sides. Fold one long edge over about four inches, thus showing both edges of fringe. Starting at the back, with the folded edge toward the neck and the fringe outside, throw one end over the left shoulder. Bring the rest around under the right arm so that the folded edge is waist-high, cross in front and toss the remainder over the left shoulder. A more common person would drape his shawl in this manner, omitting the fold and putting fringe only on one long side, which, when draped, should be at the bottom.

An Assyrian queen might wear her shawl in the following fashion. With the fringe only on one long

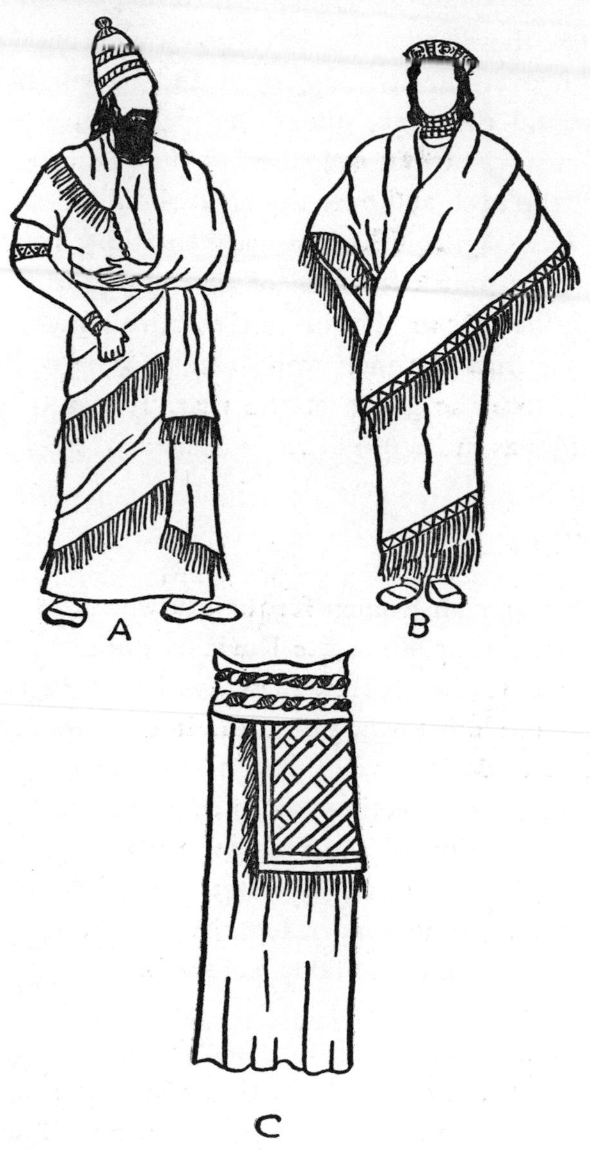

Figure 6—A and B: Draping of the fringed shawl for Assyrian king and queen. C: The use of the small square shawl for Assyrian male.

side, start the shawl at the left hip, cross in back, around in front, over the left hip again and fasten. Bring the rest around the back, under the right arm and diagonally across the front, over the left shoulder, around the back of the neck and over the right shoulder toward the front. (See Figure 6B.) The garment thus formed does not give too much freedom of movement, but the dignity of the queen should not require much activity.

Sometimes the men wore a small square shawl depended from the girdle at the rear. It was fringed on three sides as in Figure 6C.

Grecian

The Grecian women frequently wore the *himation* (hĭ-măt'ĭ-ŏn) over either the Doric or Ionic chiton. This was similar to the Hebrew shawl, which was a rectangular piece of cloth thrown over the left shoulder, around the back, under the right arm and again over the left shoulder. It was sometimes worn over the head as shown in the illustration of the Hebrew woman in Figure 7. The himation, however, was often bordered. It also was sometimes worn in longer lengths so that it could be worn twice around the body before being thrown over the left shoulder.

Another method of wearing the himation was to fold over on the outside a section of about four inches before draping in the manner just described. The folded edge was at the top. Another arrangement was to throw the remaining part of the himation over the left forearm instead of the left shoulder. Obviously this would not

Figure 7—The use of the overdrape on a New Testament woman.

do for a character that had to be active in a production. Still another and even simpler method of wear was to place the center of the himation under the left arm so that the rest of the material could be fastened together on the right shoulder with a brooch, allowing what remained of the himation to hang down front and back. One of the shorter pieces of cheesecloth might be used in this manner.

For the himation, one of the cheesecloth overdrapes described earlier may be used. The material will seem heavier if two thicknesses are used instead of the transparent single thickness. If a border is desired, just baste

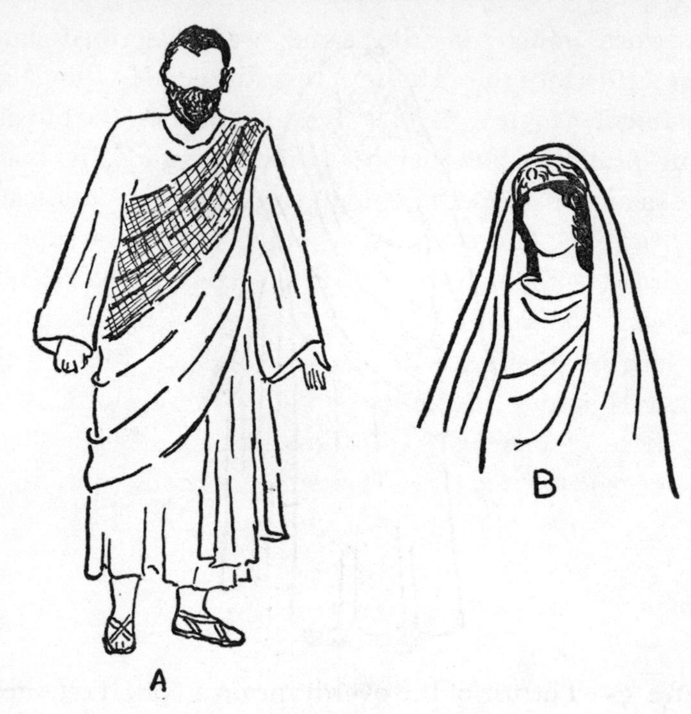

Figure 8—A: Draping of Greek chlamys or mantle. B: A Roman palla.

on a strip of three-inch contrasting color around the four sides. The border may also carry a painted design.

The men wore a mantle or *chlamys* (klā'mĭs, klăm'ĭs), which was a rectangular piece of cloth thrown about the shoulders and fastened on the left side of the neck, forming a capelike outer garment. Travelers especially wore the chlamys. This mantle was smaller than the himation. Historically, the mantle was sometimes large enough to reach the ground, in which case no tunic was worn. Older men, however, wore a long tunic plus the large mantle. The mantle, or chlamys, then was worn much in the same way described later (page 46) for the Hebrew overdrape of the New Testament. (Figure 9A.) It was folded over on the outside about fifteen inches before thrown around the body. The shaded part of the chlamys in Figure 8A indicates the overfold. The chlamys, whether worn as a cape or overdrape, was much wider than the Hebrew shawl. This fact, with the addition of the overfold, will necessitate two lengths of cheescloth stitched together. Making the seam fall among the folds will give the appearance of one piece of material. Two lengths of cheesecloth also are needed when a Grecian woman wears a wide himation.

Roman

The *toga* was the important item of dress worn by the Romans. This article of clothing assumed many variations in draping, from the simple to the elaborate. Often it was the only piece worn, being draped very intricately about the body. For the church or school stage, the simple draping is as effective as any of the more elaborate ones.

One of the fuller short-sleeved tunics, white if possible, should be worn under the toga. The draped sheet may be used for this tunic. The toga itself is very wide and should be white with a deep border of Roman design. Two lengths of four and one-half yards of tobacco cloth basted together the long way will provide ample material for effective draping. Place the toga on the left shoulder, leaving one end to reach almost to the ankle in front, with the bottom edge on a diagonal. The material should drape over the upper arm. Bring the toga around the back and under the right arm, throw it over the left shoulder and upper arm so that it hangs down the back, equidistant from the floor as the section down the front. The material across the chest may be rolled over at the top which will help the hanging ends attain the diagonal lines. Sew heavy metal washers in the corners of the toga to assure a dead-fold effect. Originally, the toga was half-moon in shape, with the straight edge being worn toward the neck. This, however, requires much material which can seldom be used for anything except a toga.

Over the many tunics, the Roman matron wore the *palla* (păl′å) which was similar to the Greek himation. It was almost veil-like in quality and was draped like that described for the Hebrew woman of the New Testament (page 46), except that the material thrown over the left shoulder from the front was *over* and not *under* the material which depended from the head. It also was worn over the right arm as well as under. If a coronet was worn, often the palla was draped so that it covered the head but not the coronet, allowing the lengths to fall over the shoulders and down the front, as in Figure 8B.

New Testament Hebrew

New Testament Hebrews adopted the use of the Roman toga and palla, which may be traced back through

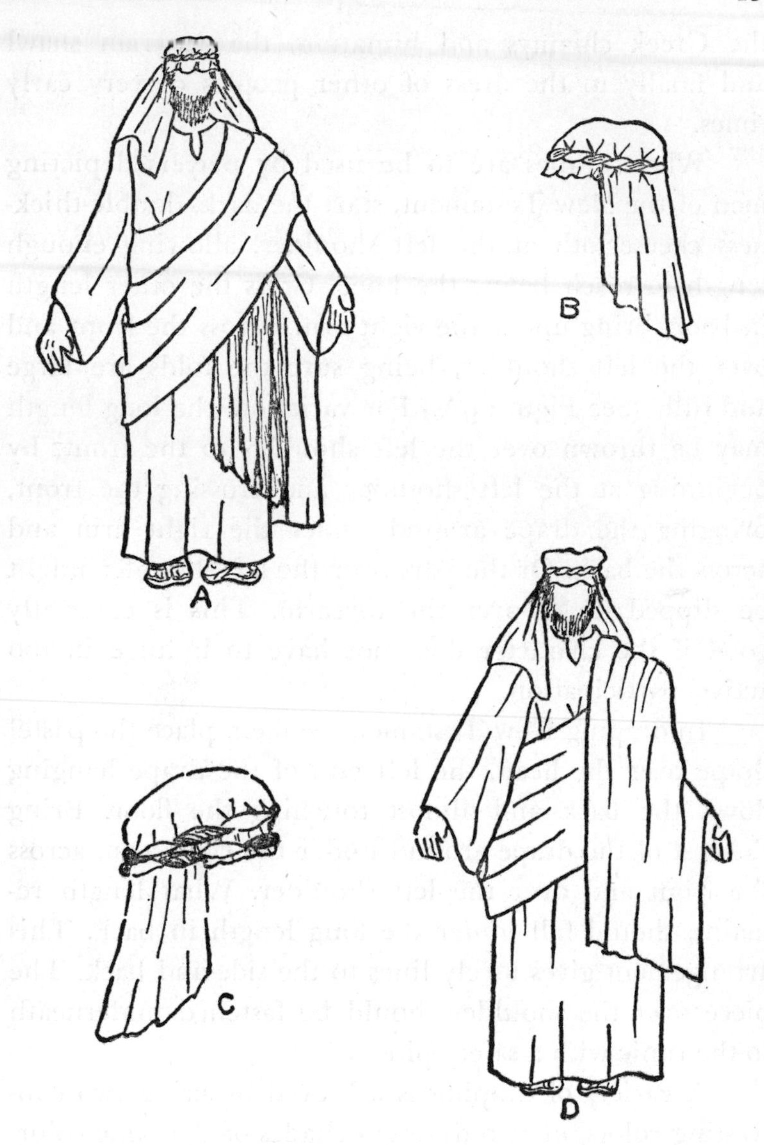

Figure 9—A and D: The use of the overdrape on a male character in the New Testament. B and C: Hebrew headdresses.

the Greek chlamys and himation, the Assyrian shawl and finally to the dress of other peoples of very early times.

When drapes are to be used by players depicting men of the New Testament, start the dark, double-thickness cheesecloth at the left shoulder, allowing enough length to reach below the knee. Cross the other length in back, bring under the right arm, across the front and over the left shoulder, being sure the folds are large and full. (See Figure 9A.) For variation, the long length may be thrown over the left shoulder to the front, by beginning at the left shoulder and crossing the front, bringing the drape around under the right arm and across the back. Or the part over the left shoulder might be slipped down over the forearm. This is especially good if the character does not have to indulge in too active participation.

In draping New Testament women, place the pastel drape over the head, the left end of the drape hanging down the back and almost touching the floor. Bring the rest of the drape around under the right arm, across the front and over the left shoulder. What length remains, should fall *under* the long length in back. This arrangement gives lovely lines to the side and back. The piece over the shoulder should be fastened underneath to the tunic with a safety pin.

A variety of draping is achieved by using two contrasting colors, or two different shades of the same color. For instance, orange and powder blue are quite effective if used together, as are light and dark green, purple and orchid, light yellow and green, or yellow and orchid.

When using two colors together in this manner, place the lengths of the drapes one upon the other, but offsetting the widths by about five or six inches. Before throwing over the head, fold the lighter shade over the darker width of the offset, or vice versa. It all depends upon the effect desired. The folds hanging down the back show the different shades and the effect is quite colorful.

In order to keep the drape from slipping from the head, first fasten a narrow ribbon or band of dark material around the head. Throw the drape over the head so that it covers the eyes. With common pins, secure the drape to the band of cloth. Then toss the drape back from the eyes so that the pins are covered. The drape will be secure and there will be no need for holding the neck stiff in order to keep the drape from slipping; and a carefully careless effect is attained. By all means, bobby pins never should be used to hold the drape in place on the head. They are very conspicuous.

The Headdress

Because the modern haircut of men is difficult to disguise and most groups can not afford even rented wigs, headdresses, especially for Hebrew characters, are quite necessary. The commonly pictured Hebrew headdress will be discussed first because of the adaptability of its two parts to other items of dress.

Hebrew

There were two parts to the Hebrew headdress, the kerchief and the tire. The kerchief is the large piece of cloth that covers the head and falls over the shoulders. The tire is a twisted piece of cloth that holds the kerchief in place. Sometimes the tire was made of goat's hair, sometimes of colorful cloth. The kerchief is at least thirty inches square; the tire may be of varying lengths and thickness, but fits the head snugly. For the Hebrew, the kerchief and tire may be worn in the following manner.

Place the kerchief over the head so that a straight edge comes just above the brows. Wind the tire around the head an inch from the edge of the kerchief which is over the forehead. Tie the tire either at the back or bring the ends around and tuck them in at the sides. The kerchief should hang loosely over the shoulders and down the back. This part of the headdress was a protection against the sand and also the sun, the nape of the neck being a vulnerable part of the body for sunstroke. The ancients must have been cognizant of this fact because all races wearing headdresses in hot climates wore material long enough to cover the nape of the neck.

The sides of the kerchief should not fall down, partially concealing the face, but should be tucked under the tire to form a right angle at the temple so that the profile is clear. This was not the usual way headdresses were worn because greater protection against the sun and sand was needed. However, the audience must be considered and a covered profile is never very interesting. A thirty-inch-square piece of cloth is the smallest that will give the right effect. Anything smaller looks skimpy. White linen napkins were used in one production, and the stiff cloth stuck out in little ruffles around the back of the neck, giving the appearance of old-fashioned dustcaps. Naturally, the effect was in deep contrast to what was intended. Figure 9B shows the conventional Hebrew headdress.

A double tire was sometimes worn, as in Figure 9C. Also, to relieve the monotony, two pieces of different colored cloth were twisted together as in Figure 9B.

Cheesecloth, tobacco cloth, sateen or flannelette, dyed any of the pastel or darker shades, make colorful headdresses. Discarded square scarfs are excellent for kerchiefs if the pattern is not too prominent and clear-cut. The kerchief often does triple duty, in that it may be used as a kerchief, a tire, or a girdle on different occasions. If it is used as a tire, make a triangle of the cloth. Starting at the right-angle point, roll the material down to the folded edge, then loosely twist the whole roll. This gives a large effective tire.

The Hebrews also wore caps and shapeless brimmed hats. However, to the average audience of a school or church play, if these caps and hats are worn in addition to the kerchief-headdresses with which they are more familiar, the suggestion is brought to mind that the costume department was forced to use makeshift. The easily

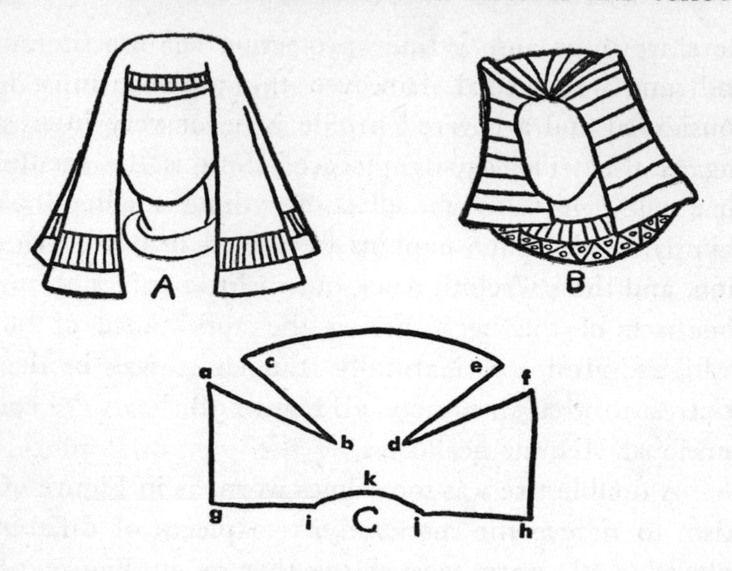

Figure 10—A and B: Egyptian headdresses. C: Pattern for cardboard foundation.

recognized kerchief and tire would eliminate any possibility of calling unwanted attention to what might appear as incongruity of costume.

The third duty of the kerchief will be discussed under the section on girdles.

Egyptian

The Hebrew kerchief may also be used for the Egyptian headdress but is arranged differently. Two methods are given here. The simplest way is first to tie a band of cloth around the head, about an inch above the brows. Over this throw one of the kerchiefs, preferably with half-inch stripes basted horizontally on the material. At the sides, just back of the ears, fasten the kerchief to the band. This makes the cloth appear to continue on around the head and to be fastened under the rest of the material. The right-angle overfold at the ears, plus the snug-fitting kerchief across the forehead assume the Egyptian look, as differentiated from the Hebrew headdress with the tire. Sometimes the ears were visible, or sometimes covered as in Figure 10A.

The second method, a little more elaborate, is to place the kerchief over a cardboard foundation. Following are the steps in making this type of headdress. Figure 10C shows a cardboard foundation, with the half-moon *ij* fitting the forehead of the wearer. Lap *ab* over *cb,* and *fd* over *de* and fasten with gummed tape. This pulls the foundation into shape, forming little cat-ears at *a* and *f*. Sew an elastic band on the wrong side of the half-moon *ij,* then bring the elastic around the back to fit the head. The foundation then has a diadem effect with sections *gi* and *jh* flaring like wings.

Fit one of the Hebrew kerchiefs over the foundation so that the kerchief assumes its shape. If the cardboard is not too heavy, this may be done with straight pins. To effect the Egyptian appearance, sew small horizontal stripes on the kerchief that covers the wing-parts and stripes radiating over the top from point *k* as shown in Figure 10B. The material falling over the wing-parts should be at least shoulder length or a little longer.

There were many different kinds of headdresses but these two are more readily recognized by the average audience as typically Egyptian. They are also more attractive.

The Egyptians were expert wigmakers, although to our standards their wigs were not too becoming as head apparel. The artificiality of them was quite apparent, as though the wigs were made that way on purpose, yarn being used instead of hair. If a wig is desired, it may be made in the following manner. The top of a black cotton stocking will fit the head snugly. Enough length should be left to cover the entire head. Gather the cut end so that a skull cap is formed. Using this cap as a base, sew black wool to it in layers, starting at the bottom and continuing to the top. This means that with each layer the wool should be cut in longer lengths to give the impression of hair growing from the scalp. For stage purposes, the hair on the completed wig only needs to be a couple of inches longer than shoulder length. Quite often the Egyptian wig was a heavy mass of hair falling over the shoulders and reaching the waist. The Egyptians were a very immaculate people, the heads of the men being shaved and the women wearing their hair short. The wigs, therefore, were a familiar part of their dress. The wig and headdress were protections against the rays of the sun.

Assyrian

The nonroyal Assyrian male wore a turbanlike headdress as in Figure 11A. This may be made from cardboard and be left white or colored dark green, old rose or dusky purple. (The term "dusky" as used in this text refers to a color with a mixture of gray, giving it a subdued shade that will easily blend with almost any other

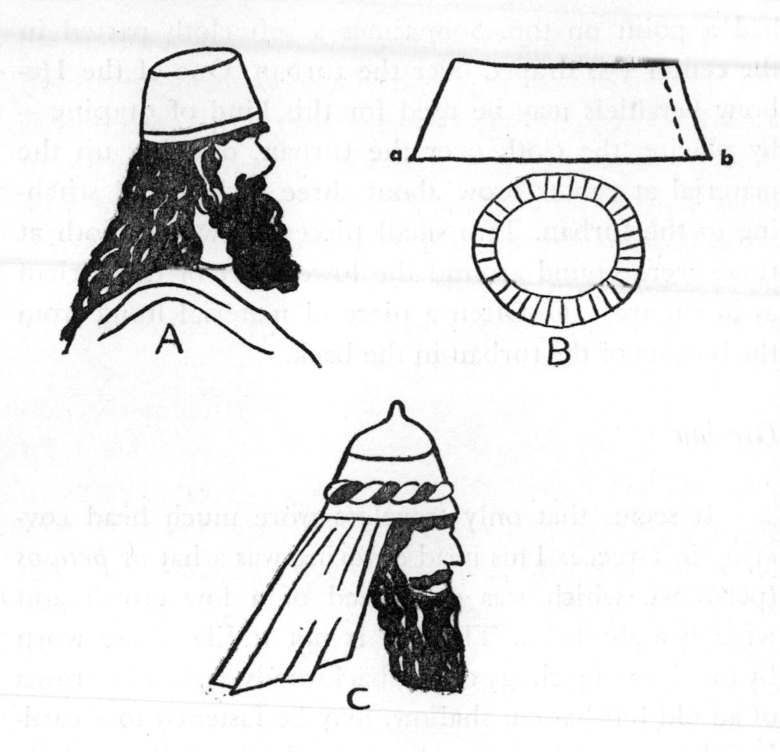

Figure 11—A: Assyrian male turban. B: Pattern for cardboard foundation. C: Assyrian royalty turban.

color.) The cardboard is in two pieces, as in Figure 11B. The elongated piece extending from *a* to *b* should fit the wearer's head, measuring from just above the brows and on around, allowing an extra inch, indicated by the dotted line, to be glued to the other end. The circular top piece is an inch larger than the top of the cone so that it may be slit at half-inch intervals. Bend these tabs to fit inside the cone, and glue.

Royalty wore a more elaborate turban which always

had a point on top. Sometimes a soft cloth parted in the center was draped over the turban. One of the Hebrew kerchiefs may be used for this kind of draping—by placing the cloth over the turban, drawing up the material at center brow about three inches, and stitching to the turban. Two small pieces of twisted cloth at times were bound around the lower part of the turban as in Figure 11C. Often a piece of material hung from the bottom of the turban in the back.

Grecian

It seems that only travelers wore much head covering in Greece. This head covering was a hat or *petasos* (pĕt′å-sŏs), which was comprised of a low crown and wide straight brim. The hat is not unlike those worn by the traveling clergy of our backwoods days. The crown of an old felt hat cut shallow, may be fastened to a cardboard brim with strips of gummed paper. The whole object is painted navy blue. This camouflaged petasos need not be worn but may be carried if the action in the play does not demand that the character wear it. In fact, for the sake of eliminating any humorous reaction, it might be well if it *were* carried, or at least left hanging down the back from a string around the neck. According to our present-day standards, the petasos is not an especially flattering piece of wearing apparel.

To be authentic as to hairdress, the men wore their beards and hair in long formal curls. Even at this early date, heated irons were used. If it is desired that a character wear the long curls, a wig is necessary.

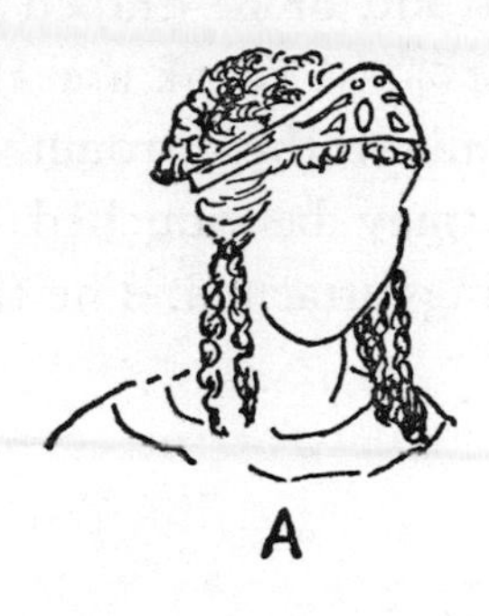

Figure 12—Greek diadems.

The women parted their hair in the middle, brought it down over the ears and caught it up in back in curls secured with a ribbon or *fillet* (fĭl′ĕt). One or two of the curls hung down over the shoulders. Low curls were also worn over the forehead. Sometimes the hair was worn in a "Psyche knot" and bands placed around the head to hold the hair firmly in place. Diadems or crownlike headdresses were worn. (See Figures 12A and 12B.)

Roman

The Roman women also wore coronets, or crownlike headdresses, placed high on the forehead. The coronets should be about three inches high in front and taper to about one inch at the back of the head. A headdress of this kind could be made of cardboard and painted gold. Over this, so that the coronet shows, is thrown the palla. (See Figure 8B.) It may fall in folds over the shoulders and down the front, or be draped in the simple manner described under "The Cloak and the Overdrape" in this section. To adapt the coronet to different head-sizes, a small hole may be punched in each end of the cardboard, and strings attached. The ties will fall under the palla.

The Girdle

Girdles worn in a variety of ways were necessary items of clothing. They consisted of wide leather belts, cloth belts three to four inches in width, narrow, rope-like bands, or long sashes and ribbons.

Hebrew

One type of beltlike leather girdle which was worn extensively by the Hebrew people was at least four inches wide. In this were pockets for money, possibly worn on the side next to the body. Money bags and knives were tucked inside the belts. The wealthier classes often wore semiprecious stones on the leather. Some girdles were very ornate, others quite simply studded, depending upon the wealth and rank of the wearer.

The belt may be made from imitation leather or heavy cardboard. If cardboard is used, it should be painted brown to simulate leather. To make the stones, colored cellophane may be attached to the belt in the following manner.

Punch small holes in the girdle wherever the stones

are to be placed. Cut the cellophane into four-inch squares. Then gather together the four corners and edges of each square and force them through the holes, care being taken not to tear the material of the girdle. The cellophane remaining on the outside should not be less than one-half inch across. It will definitely be in a crumpled condition, which is correct because it will catch and reflect the lights better, and sparkle more like a jewel. To relieve any uncomfortable scratching, some of the ends should be clipped on the inside, and the rest of the material spread out and flattened. Red, green, yellow and blue cellophane may be used for the stones.

To fasten the girdle, punch a row of small holes at each end of the cardboard. Notebook-hole reinforcers used on both inside and out will help keep the holes from tearing. These should be put on before the cardboard is painted leather-brown. Lace brown shoestrings, with metal tips removed, through the holes and tie at the bottom. The lacing may be in the back or under one arm.

Long scarves are suitable for the cloth girdles, which were worn extensively. The material should have enough body to retain a width of three to four inches. Plain colors are desirable, but stripes are permissible. The ends should not hang down but should be crossed in back, pinned inconspicuously, and tucked in the sides.

The third use of the kerchief of the headdress, mentioned earlier, may be employed here—as a girdle—if no other girdle is available. If possible, two kerchiefs of the same color should be used. One alone is likely to crush into a skimpy, ropelike girdle, which for stage use is never very impressive. In any case, for the Hebrew girdle, the material should not be too soft, and should be at least three inches wide. It should not look like a rag tied around the middle. Fold the kerchief into a triangle. Turn the right-angle corner down four inches, then turn the folded edge up another four inches and continue until four inches of girdle is obtained. This may have to be pinned in the back if it is not long enough to tie.

Assyrian

The Assyrian girdle for the men was distinctive in that it consisted of two pieces. The larger, probably made of leather, was from three to four inches wide. It was held in place by a narrow girdle about an inch wide, wound twice around the waist. Through the girdle often one or two daggers or knives were thrust as in Figure 13A. Again cardboard or heavy cloth, such as unbleached muslin, may be used for the wide part of the girdle.

Grecian

The women of Sparta and the country surrounding that city were more athletic than the women found elsewhere in Greece, and thus often wore the chiton shorter. The shorter the chiton, the longer the overfold. In this case, the girdle was frequently placed over the overfold which extended several inches below the waist; the kol-

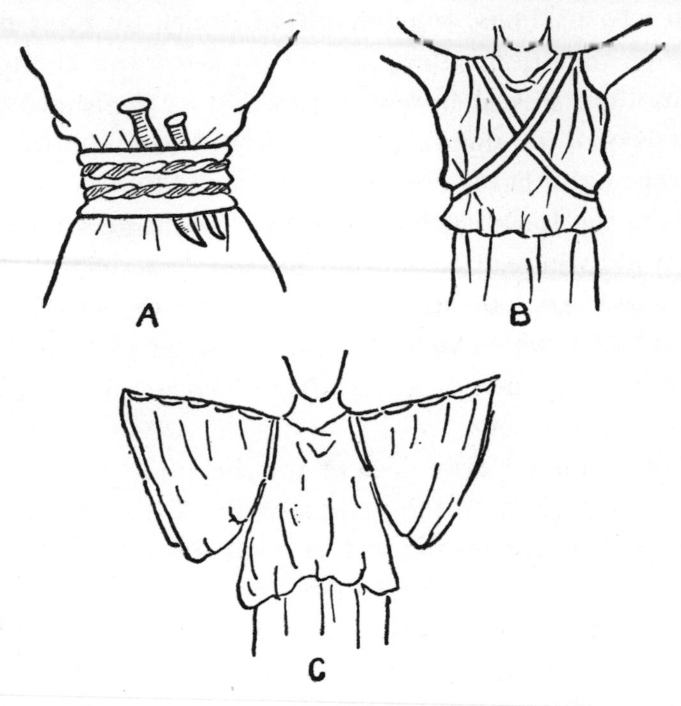

Figure 13—A: Assyrian girdle. B: Doric girdle. C: Ionic girdle.

pos, or bloused effect, about six or eight inches below that. Greater freedom of movement was achieved with this kind of arrangement. The "peplos of Athena" was effected in this manner. However, the entire length of the chiton for the "peplos of Athena" reached to the ankles. The Dorians also wore a double-girded chiton, using an unconcealed girdle at the waist and a second girdle around the hips to form the kolpos. This second girdle was not in evidence.

Another method of girding was effected by the use of a narrow ribbon in addition to the girdle at the waist. This ribbon was sometimes placed at the back, a couple of inches above the girdle, each end brought around and crossed in front, thrown over the shoulders and secured to the first piece in the rear. This was typical of the Doric chiton as shown in Figure 13B.

On the Ionic chiton, the ribbon was drawn around the armpits instead of crossing in front. The ribbon for both types kept the chiton in place on the shoulders. The ribbon, which helped form the sleeves of the full Ionic chiton, was not always in evidence. (See Figure 13C.)

Still another arrangement for the Ionic chiton was to place the girdle at the natural waistline and draw the material up and over, until it hung in a long pouch effect halfway to the knees. This was not like the Doric chiton, because the Ionic had no overfold. A curved kolpos often was formed at the hips by pulling up the chiton so that it was even at the hem. If a kolpos is desired, the material of the chiton should indeed be thin and soft, otherwise bulkiness will be the result.

Roman

To make the girdle for a Roman woman, use a two-inch ribbon three yards in length. Place it high-waisted in front, bring it around and cross in back, over each shoulder to the front, around the armpits and tie in back. Tie a second ribbon at least three yards long around the hips and allow to fall in front. Over this second girdle, the short tunic is pulled up to form the bloused effect.

The Sandal

The foot should be covered for several reasons. One reason again is that of humor. Unfortunately, most audiences have not been educated to look upon the bare foot on the stage as a typical part of the costumes of the ancients, except in the character of Jesus, which is not often portrayed in amateur productions. Although to be authentic, Abraham, Moses and many other Biblical characters should go unshod, the humor of seeing an acquaintance or close friend traipsing around in bare feet on the amateur stage is often too much for the average neighborhood audience. The spell of the scene is usually lost in a ripple of amusement. Another reason for covering the foot is that most amateur actors object to going barefoot through self-consciousness, or through fear of catching cold if the presentation is in winter.

So it is better for the feet to be covered, but not with twentieth-century shoes! Clomping around in heavy-soled Oxfords or tapping along in high-heeled slippers is hardly the way to convince an audience that the characters which are being portrayed are the Prophet Isaiah or the Mother of Jesus. Inconsistency in costume is always to be avoided, even though it is thought that "the audience will never notice it." Shoes should be replaced by the sandals of Biblical times.

Even though the production has many characters, the task of making sandals for all should be undertaken. Most members of the cast are capable of making their own, as was done by the players in a large production in Cleveland, Ohio, a short time ago. There were hundreds in the cast, which appeared before an audience of ten thousand, but not one character was allowed on the stage in modern footwear. To have rented sandals for everyone was financially prohibitive and for the costume committee to have made them would have indeed been a chore. In a production of this size, the cast was instructed to make its own. Some in the populace scenes chose to go barefoot, which was all right since they mingled easily with the rest of the cast.

Sandals are not difficult to make. If they need not be used again, a one- or two-night-stand type of sandal may be made from inner soles or corrugated cardboard, cut to the shape of the particular foot, or rounded at the toes. Cut the material not more than a quarter of an inch larger than the foot. Any material smaller or just the same size is likely to expose parts of the foot to the bare floor. If it is made any larger than a quarter of an inch, the wearer may catch the protruding piece either in his long garments or on the edge of any steps he has to use. Long, flowing robes in themselves are difficult to manage without adding the hazards of oversized sandals.

Lace strips of dark cloth through slits in the cardboard near the toes so that one length comes between the first and second toe, the other length between the fourth and fifth toe, or wherever it is comfortable. Cross these two lengths first over the toes before taking them under the instep of the cardboard. Bring up and cross once more over the instep, and down under the heel.

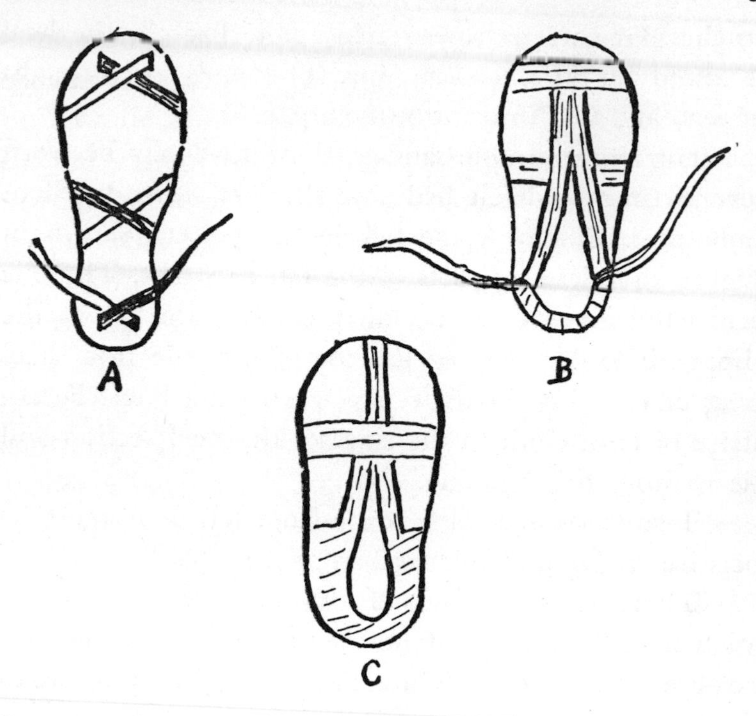

Figure 14—Sandals.

Then bring up through two slits at the heel, crossing the straps at the back and tieing in front of the ankle. Strapping the sandal in this fashion helps keep the cardboard from cracking and holds it firmly to the foot. Figure 14A illustrates this type of sandal.

Sometimes the inner-sole or cardboard sandals are more securely held on the feet by sewing wide strips of dark cloth across the toes and over the instep immediately below the ankle. These strips are stitched on the bottom of the sole with heavy thread and large stitches. Often a narrower strip at the back of the heel is sewed on in the same way. The ends are brought around and tied in front of the ankle.

For more durable sandals, those that may be worn several times, old felt bedroom slippers make excellent imitations. Cut away the felt in the pattern shown in Figure 14B, leaving parts of the felt as straps. The one across the toes should be fairly close to the tip of the slipper in order to keep the toe of the sole from flapping or catching on uneven places in the floor. Fasten strips of dark cloth to the sides of the heel section and tie in front of the ankle.

Two types of sandals made from felt bedroom slippers are shown in Figures 14B and 14C.

There are some kinds of soft-soled beach and recreation slippers which may be used as they are. However, no "wedgies!" Not only are they dead giveaways as to the age in which they are worn, but also clumsy in use and awkward in appearance.

Sandals in Figures 14B and 14C may be worn by any character being portrayed in Biblical times. They are indefinite enough in appearance not to call attention to themselves.

For a change, Assyrian hunters often wore boots, widely laced horizontally in front. Sew a cloth, wide enough to encase the sides of the leg and long enough to reach below the knee, to the basic sandal. Leave the front open except for the lacing.

Heavy woolen socks dyed leather brown make excellent Roman boots. Long dark-brown shoelaces stitched up the front of the sock to resemble actual lacings change the appearance of the sock immeasurably, especially if the sock is also turned down about an inch at the top. Often the leather boots were decorated. To simulate this effect, dark brown or black showcard paint may be applied in broken and indefinite patterns on the sides, back and toe of the boot. Heavy cardboard may be stitched to the soles of the sock to insure more durability.

High leather boots were worn in Greece by the country folk. Sandals laced over the instep were worn more by the town people.

The Roman Soldier

The Roman soldier often makes his appearance in Biblical drama, especially in the New Testament plays, so a special section will be devoted here to the making of his armor and accouterments.

The Armor

Some authorities say the armor was of heavy leather instead of the conventional Passion-play armor of metal. Of course, the latter is more spectacular and better known to audiences, but according to these authorities, the Passion-play armor did not come into being until a couple of centuries after the birth of Christ, a leather foundation being used instead with metal pieces attached.

However, if you wish to use the all-metal armor

(and perhaps your audience would accept it as more authentic than any other), it is not too difficult to make.

From unbleached muslin cut a straight piece of material large enough to encase the body from upper chest to waist. At the top, cut out half-circles to fit under the arms. At one end, allow for an underfold of four inches for fastening at one side or in the back. With this underfold and using plenty of large hooks and eyes, no gapping will occur. Sometimes leather thongs were used to hold the armor together at the sides. If this type of fastening is desired, long brown shoelaces with the metal tips removed may be used. From muslin, cut the shoulder pieces one and a half inches in width. The number of pieces needed depends upon the width of the character's shoulders, and the pieces when put together should be no wider. Sew these pieces together and round the ends, which should overlap the breastplate about two inches front and back. Sewing the shoulder pieces to the breastplate will hold the entire armor together securely.

Cover the whole piece of armor with aluminum paint. Paint broken, narrow horizontal lines in black around the armor, not less than three inches apart. This gives the appearance of strips of metal being used instead of one large piece. If leather thongs are not used for fastening at the side, paint curves on each strip down the middle of the front and insert paper fasteners in the center of each curve to resemble lengths of metal strips riveted together. A similar impression is made with the shoulder pieces. Sometimes the shoulder pieces are made in three strips with a "rivet" at each end.

Another method of making armor is to start again with the undyed muslin foundation and glue on two-inch strips of heavy wrapping paper or gummed tape. Cover this with aluminum paint. Paint on paper has a tendency to reflect the light more brightly than paint on muslin. One disadvantage with this type of armor is that it will rustle if not glued properly. However, the clank of the chains that hold the swords quite often covers any noise the paper makes.

Still another way is to use suit-box cardboard, cutting it in strips three inches wide. Overlap these in front and rivet with paper fasteners, punched through and spread on the inside. Secure the strips together on the inside with gummed paper. Bind the pieces over the shoulder together in the same way so that they do not spread, and rivet to the breastplate or tie with leather thongs. Cover the whole armor with aluminum paint. If rivets are not used in front, lace together the front and back sections of the armor at the side.

For contrast and to add a little rank so as to make the armor that of a centurion, glue strips of the "brown-leather" muslin to the lower edge of the armor, which rests on the hips. The strips should be eight inches long and four inches wide, rounded on the ends. The ends of the tabs may be painted with the aluminum paint to give an appearance of metal. The soldier in Figure 15A shows the addition of these strips, which thus change the legionnaire's armor to that of a centurion.

Under the armor is worn a short-sleeved tunic of dark color, brown or dark gray. The tunic reaches no farther than the knees, usually just above.

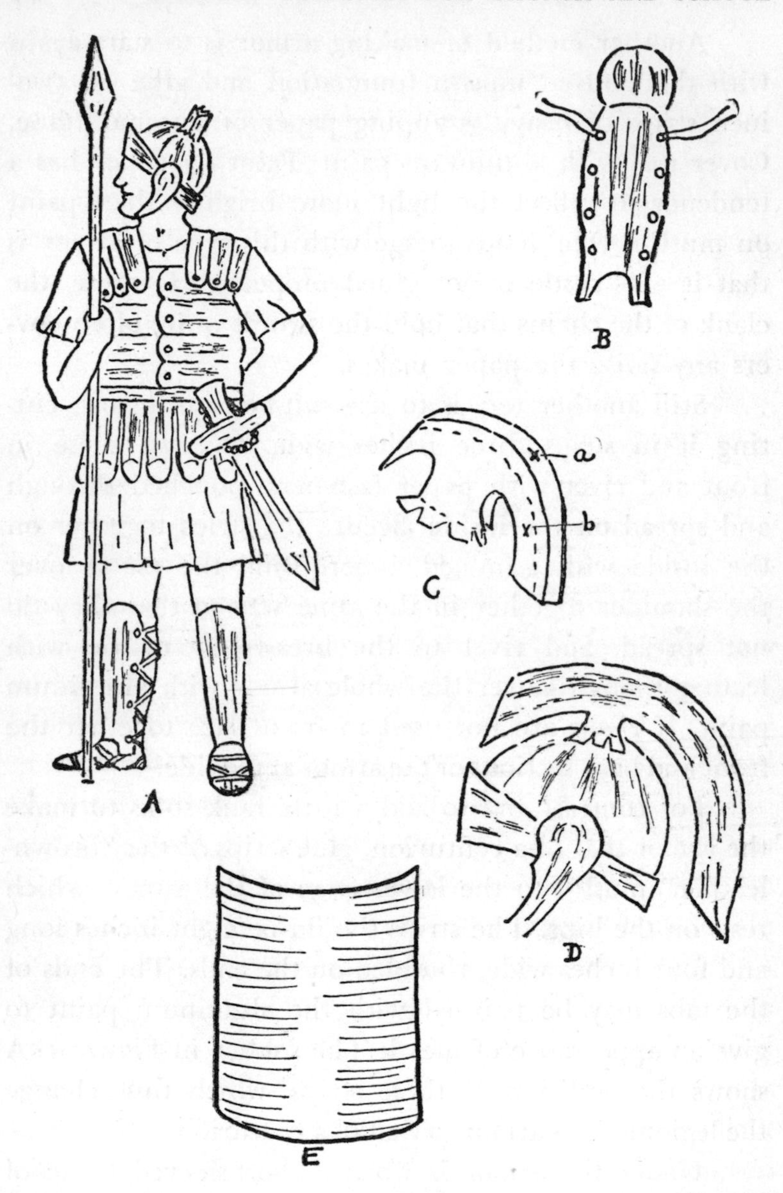

Figure 15—Roman armor with patterns for different parts.

Men wearing this kind of armor should have the typical physique of Roman soldiers. They were a rugged lot. No esthetic-looking bookworm will appear as though he were able to stand the rigors of the Roman military life. Thin arms and legs, hollow chests, only evoke amusement on the part of the audience. If there is no man of sturdy physique in the group to take this part, strike out the part or discard the play. The soldier should not be subjected to ridicule.

The Shinguard

Shinguards, called greaves by the Greek warriors, may also be worn by the Roman soldier, since Roman dress was greatly influenced by that of the Greeks. These are easily made from suit-box cardboard. Cut the guards to fit the shin below the knee to the ankle. Curve the top and cut out the bottom to fit over the angle formed by the foot and leg. Small two-inch extensions cover the ankle bones. The guards go only halfway around the leg. They are held on by dark strips of cloth fastened through holes at the top, laced through a couple of holes down the sides and tied at the bottom.

The centurion's shinguards may be made a little more elaborate by adding a rounded "cap" of cardboard that covers the knees. Cover all shinguards with aluminum paint and lightly streak with black to add shadows and take away the appearance of newness, as in Figure 15B.

The Helmet

Helmets are necessary items for the outfits of Roman soldiers and should be described here. Crowns of old felt hats make excellent foundations upon which to add the different little pieces that transform them from modern headwear to that of ancient Rome.

Make the visor and neckguard from cardboard. Cut the visor in coronet fashion, about four inches at center front, tapering down to about one and one-half inches at the sides. The neckguard is similar in shape but not as wide; about two and one-half inches is allowed for the widest part of the neckguard. At the sides of the crown sew these two pieces with large stitches, end to end, attaching them to the felt-hat foundation. At this point, place the eartabs. Actually they were pieces of metal, hinged to the side and tied under the chin with leather strips. The same effect may be made from pieces of muslin about three and one-half inches wide at the top, tapering to about one inch under the chin. To sew it to the helmet, place the wide end at the upper side of the joined ends of the visor and neckguard, throwing the chin-end over the top of the hat. The piece is now upside-down. Sew with large horizontal stitches to the helmet just above the cardboard. Bring the muslin down so the stitches do not show. In this way, the straps cover the point of jointure of the neckguard and visor. The straps are held in place under the chin with hook and eye or shoelace "leather" strips. The leather strips make the straps immediately adjustable to the wearer. Chin pieces may be made of thin cardboard but muslin is a little more comfortable to wear and more easily managed in the making. Note the crown, visor and earlaps in Figure 15D.

Directly on top of the helmet in Figure 15A is an ornamental piece. This, too, is made of cardboard. It is six and one-half inches long and three and one-fourth inches wide. With a pencil, divide the length into four one-and-one-half-inch sections. There will be a one-half inch section left over. Each section should be pointed so that together the four look like a picket fence with no space between the boards. Draw a line one-half inch from the bottom and cut each section apart as high as the line. This will allow the sections to be bent in the shape of a hollow cube with a flared bottom. Glue the half inch that is left over behind the section that it meets. Stitch the four flared pieces at the bottom to the top of the helmet, making the ornament stand upright.

Figure 15C shows a pattern for the crest of the centurion's helmet. It is made in three sections, the top, *a,* and two sides, *b,* with flared bottoms like the legionnaire's. The top section is a straight piece of cardboard with extended sides which are slit at one-inch intervals and bent to fasten on the reverse of the side pieces. The flared bottoms are stitched to the top of the helmet.

Now the whole helmet is ready for aluminum paint, the muslin eartabs included. More than one coat may be needed, especially on the felt. After the paint has thoroughly dried, the helmet will be quite stiff, but will hold its shape and give the appearance of metal.

In order to take away the painted look as well as the impression that the armor was purchased only the day before, quite often black paint is very lightly brushed across the visor and neckguard. As in the case of the breastplate, this also gives the illusion of shadows, which makes the armor more interesting.

The Belt

The costume is not yet quite complete. A plain, modern, dark leather belt is needed. To this on the left side is attached a short series of chain links, through which the broadsword is thrust. These pieces of chain may be purchased at most hardware stores, or made from thin lead strips. Lead bends easily, and links from three-and-one-half-inch lengths may be formed.

The Sword and Knife

Since the sword and knife are seldom used to run through a character in a Biblical production, they may be made of wood. In the broadsword of the Roman soldier, the blade is usually quite wide, about four inches, and pointed at the end. The edges are filed and tapered with a wood rasp so that they look sharp. The length of the sword usually is about two feet and has a wide hilt spliced into the blade. (See Figure 16A.) The whole instrument is covered with aluminum paint. The sword for a Roman officer might be longer and not quite so wide. This helps differentiate him from the Roman legionnaire. (See Figure 16B.)

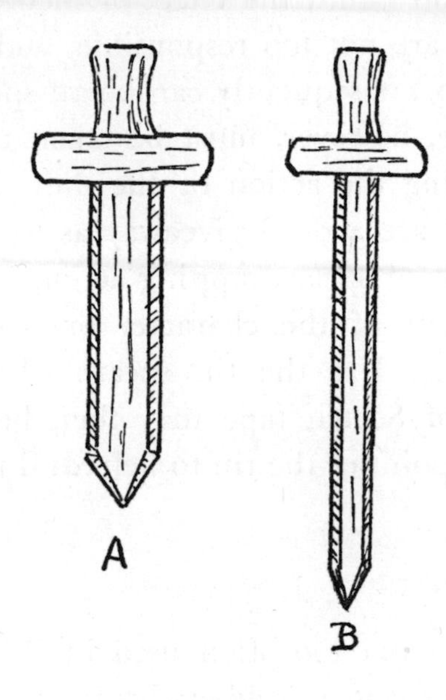

Figure 16—Roman swords.

Knives may be made in the same manner, with six-inch-long blades about one inch in width. The hilts are small, and the narrow handles either curved or straight.

The Spear

If spears are used, they should be at least six feet long, not counting the point. The spearheads themselves should measure ten inches and may be made from coffee cans. The tin flashes very realistically under lights but can be dangerous if not handled carefully. It is better to eliminate any possibility of injuring someone by making spearheads of heavy show-card paper. By using aluminum paint, the effect of metal is adequate. Young people are not too responsible, and often adults are even less so, consequently cardboard spears are more desirable. Care, however, must be taken not to let the spear fall during the action or the dull thud of wood and cardboard are a dead giveaway as to the construction. If this bit of spear-dropping action is necessary to the development of the character or story, that is a different matter. Use the tin spearheads; and a very narrow strip of Scotch tape may then be folded over the edges and point of the tin to help dull the sharpness.

The Shield

Shields are not too often used in Biblical productions employing Roman soldiers because Roman soldiers usually are not shown in battle formation. Both hands were more often needed to hold spears, which the soldiers used as barriers when handling a crowd rather than as weapons in inflict injury, so shields would definitely be in the way.

If a shield is needed, use heavy cardboard—a rectangular piece about thirty inches wide and forty inches long. To make the outside convex in shape, fasten pieces of cloth from corner to corner at top and bottom and one across center, about seven inches from the rim. The length of these should be just short enough to make the amount of curve that is desired. The shield should be only slightly curved to afford protection around the body, as in Figure 15E.

The shields had two straps on the inside, one to

be grasped by the hand, the other to go over the arm just below the elbow. Since individual arms are of different lengths, this fact would make the shield quite a personal piece of equipment.

The Sandal

The soldier should wear sandals. Those in Figure 14B are adequate.

The Accessories

From paintings, statuettes, pottery and the like, and from tombs which have been discovered, much has been learned about the accessories of the people living in Biblical times. Bracelets, anklets, necklaces, earrings, pins, in fact jewelry of all kinds, were extensively worn. Adapting ancient jewelry to the stage is relatively simple. At the present writing, some costume jewelry has been copied from the heavy, ornate pieces worn by the Egyptians, Assyrians, Greeks and Romans. These are especially well adapted for use on the stage. In the first place they are large, a fact that should be kept in mind when ornamenting costumes with designs or using jewelry of any kind.

In lieu of costume jewelry, the arm bands worn by the many ancient peoples may be simulated by the use of cardboard cut to fit the arm of the wearer. They should be at least two inches wide. The ends are fastened together by very small elastic bands so that the arm bands may slip easily over the hands and elbows, if worn that high, and stay in place on the arms. Gold paint is applied and lightly brushed with black to give the appearance of wrought gold. Indefinite designs may be made with the black paint, which also helps the illusion that the bands are made of metal.

Macaroni cut in varying lengths and painted with heavy showcard paint make interesting necklaces and embroidery. Pieces of curled or elbow macaroni also are effective.

Colored cellophane, arranged in design on a cardboard backing, makes medallions and pendants. Strips of colored cellophane may also be sewn in a design on a muslin backing for the elaborate Egyptian collars. These collars were made to lie flat and fit snugly around the neck, and on them was brightly colored embroidery. It consisted of thread, beads, enamel or precious stones, depending upon the wealth and rank of the wearer.

Also narrow strips of colored cloth may be basted around the necks of tunics to simulate embroidery.

It should be kept in mind that small, delicate and intricate designs on the stage are lost. Those in the rear of the audience should be able to make out the general appearance of an ornament, whether it is jewelry or a decoration on the costume itself. Decorations on clothing maintain the same principle applied to the painting of scenery. Lines are not complete. Completed lines stand out too boldly, and look stiff and artificial. This is especially true on a small stage or where the characters are close to the audience. On a larger stage, the uncompleted lines may be exaggerated in intensity and the audience-eye will fill in the missing sections. Indefinite patterns are generally more effective than patterns where painstaking detail has been exercised.

The Colors

Chaldean

The very early people were closer to the soil than those who followed. Therefore, earthy shades were predominant. Rust-red, brown, ochre-yellow, dark indigo blue, dusky green, and ecru should be the colors to use in the costumes of Abraham, Sarah, Isaac, Jacob, Esau, Rachel, Rebecca and others of that time.

Originally ochre was a native earth ranging from light yellow to deep orange and brown. Ochre-yellow in this instance would be a brownish-yellow, making it a strong shade of yellow, in harmony with the character of the people using it. Ecru, on the other hand, would be a yellowish-brown. Where ochre-yellow tends to lean more toward the shade of yellow than brown, the base of ecru would be brown, with a dash of yellow.

Egyptian

Vivid colors, especially in regard to decorations, were used by the Egyptians. For the collars and aprons, the following colors are appropriate: clear yellow, blue-green or emerald, vermilion (bright red, tending slightly toward orange), garnet (deep red), the different blues, and green-blue and intense violet-blue.

Material may be dyed dark or lighter indigo, red tending toward henna, ecru, dusky yellow-green, and dark wine or purple. With materials possessing these slightly heavier shades, the brilliantly colored aprons, collars and arm bands will stand out in effective contrast.

Assyrian

The Assyrians, cruel and more warlike in character than any other people of the Old Testament, used stronger colors, such as green, red, mulberry (reddish-purple), black, white, and much gold. King Solomon would be attired in a costume that followed the trend of Assyrian splendor. A choice of designs, if the budget allows, aids greatly in giving his dress a gorgeous appearance. The Assyrians used geometric designs, stripes, zigzags, and circles. There was also a "scale" pattern that was popular. Stories dealing with the reign of Babylon have the Assyrian influence, since the Assyrian and Babylonian periods merged, first with one country being in power, then the other. The Assyrian influence seems to be the stronger of the two, so that the characters of Daniel, Nebuchadnezzar, Belshazzar and other persons connected with them (although Babylon was in power at the time) may be clothed in the Assyrian manner and still be authentic.

Persian

Persia, in contrast to Assyria, for the most part used softer colors, such as yellow-green, mulberry, soft yellow, green, and red. Black, white and gold were also used but were not as outstanding as in the Assyrian dress. A vivid greenish-blue was one popular striking color. The dramatic story of Esther is effectively portrayed with the use of these colors.

Grecian

The Greeks did not employ much color except in borders and decorations. These may be made in dark purple, red, blue, black, saffron (orange), and yellow. Men of the upper classes wore the tunic and mantle of white, while the lower classes dressed more in the grays and browns. For designs, see section on "References" at end of text.

Roman

White predominates in the Roman dress, although the women also wore light, bright tones. Royalty, or those in high office, wore a white toga with a wide purple border. Lesser men wore white togas with borders in colored design, or no border at all.

Hebrew, Old Testament

Early Hebrews probably were clothed in garments using the colors suggested under "Chaldean." After that period in history, the colors were influenced by the people under whose domination the Israelites happened to be at the time.

Hebrew, New Testament

Since during this phase of their history, the Hebrew people were under the power of Rome, the garments were similar to those of the Romans. Men wore a simple adaptation of the toga but with more color. However, the colors were darker—navy blue, wine, dusky yellow, brown, gray, and dark green being those most commonly used. Brighter colors may be employed in the abas, especially in regard to the stripes. The headdresses, also, should be in brighter tones. The women copied the Greek himation and the Roman palla. Vivid colors were used on these overdrapes and in the tunics.

Adaptations

All the colors listed above are not necessarily good for stage purposes. Red, for example, is a difficult color to use. Its different shades clash more often than harmonize with each other and with other colors. Black, on the average small stage that often has inadequate lighting, is too funereal in appearance. Without exception, navy blue should be used in its place. It will give the appearance of black but will have life to it. White, in itself, is too conspicuous and the contrast too outstanding. If possible, an off-white, that with a little yellow in it, is better. If the draped sheet is used as the undergarment, it should be covered as much as possible with the overdrape, or aba.

The more vivid the colors, the more difficult it is to blend them and make attractive combinations. So, with groups who are concerned with limited budgets and wardrobes, it is better to start with pastel shades for the women and dusky tones, or darker shades, for the men. These are more easily made interchangeable and may be used for any character in any period. They blend well and do not fight each other. This is especially true in regard to small casts of four or five characters who are on the stage at the same time. The lovely pastel shades of yellow, green, orchid, blue and orange, in their contrast to the more dusky tones of the men, make an interesting Biblical scene that is easy on the audience-eye. The more vivid shades are often harsh or even brittle-looking. Occasionally, a certain type of character will require the use of these shades. However, care must be taken that the costumes of other characters do not clash with whatever outfit this particular character wears. Mary Magdalene, for instance, before her conversion, is often portrayed in a red overdrape. This is permissible if the other characters do not wear orange, orchid or certain shades of blue and purple. That, of course, limits the selection of colors. A harsh, earthy character would do well to emphasize the brilliant coloring of his decorations and accessories, rather than make the garments themselves loud and unyielding in tone.

Section Two

The Time of Abraham

Abraham and Sarah are probably the oldest characters mentioned in the Bible to be impersonated. The story of Cain and Abel might contain a little too much blood-and-thunder to dramatize among children. The garments of Cain and Abel also are scantier and more barbaric in appearance than some school or church audiences will accept. So these characters will be bypassed.

Events in the lives of Abraham and Sarah, and of Isaac, Jacob and Esau, may be enacted by young adults or adults.

Abraham and Sarah in Ur

Since Abraham and Sarah were from the city or district of Ur of the Chaldees, they wore Chaldean garments. Most peoples at that time were shepherds and farmers, thus it is quite likely that the material they wore was wool. Those in the city were dependent upon those who lived and worked close to the soil and no doubt the former also wore this material.

Research shows that Abraham was an important figure in Ur. He probably wore only a large fringed shawl, draped to cover most of his body. For the stage, however, there will no doubt have to be an undergarment or short-sleeved tunic that comes to the ankle like the one in Figure 1C. Over this the fringed shawl is draped. For this shawl, use two of the dark-colored cheesecloth overdrapes referred to on page 36. The shawl really should be four feet in width, but cheesecloth and tobacco cloth seldom come that wide. This is one reason why a tunic is needed under the shawl. For an average-sized man, the shawl, even with the fringe, is not long enough to reach the ankles. However, it is possible to sew two of the yard-wide shawls together, making the material six feet wide. With this width, a voluminous effect is achieved by draping it in the following manner.

Hold one end of the shawl under the left arm, cross in back, bring under right arm, cross in front, and under left arm again to right arm. Then throw the shawl over the left shoulder, cross in back and under right arm, and tuck into first folds in front. This leaves the right arm and shoulder bare, except for the sleeve of the tunic. At the edge of the sleeve, a three-inch metal-like arm band may be worn. Figure 17A shows how the shawl would cover the body were the tunic

Figure 17—Abraham and Sarah in Ur.

not worn. The figure here, however, wears the tunic in addition to the shawl.

Although little is known of the physique of Abraham, it is good to think of him as possessing a very sturdy figure, able to cope with the Wilderness into which he and Sarah went. If the draping of the shawl is loose, it will assist in conveying this impression. The arm band helps broaden the upper arm.

The hair should be shoulder length and the square beard should extend to the collar bone. However, Abraham may be clean-shaven. The long hair may necessitate renting a wig. The beard, if it is worn, should match the wig in color.

Abraham probably went barefoot, but early sandals may be simulated by following or varying the simplest style in Figures 14B and 14C. In his hand he may carry a staff, with the bark still on it.

If Abraham wears a headdress, a hat about five inches high, brimless, cylindrical in shape, and studded with gold-headed nails would be authentic-looking. The hat, made of cardboard, should be painted dark brown to look like leather; the gold studs may be either roundhead-brass paper fasteners punched through and spread on the inside, or painted gold dots outlined in black. The hat should fit the head of the wearer and come down to just above the tip of the ears, which will bring it across the forehead. This kind of hat should be worn with long hair, otherwise the incongruity of it with a modern haircut is ludicrous. If the hat is not to be removed, the illusion of long hair may be created by using crepe hair* fastened with spirit gum to the inside of the hat in the back.

Sarah should be simply clothed with a sleeveless tunic, over which is a scarf three yards in length. The scarf is thrown around the shoulders and upper part of the arms, crossed in front and tied in back. The scarf may be one of the darker cheesecloth overdrapes, since the colors of this period should be dark and virile-looking. (See Figure 17B.)

Instead of the scarf, a shorter rectangle with a draw-string in the length and pulled up around the neck to form a cape, may be used. The cape should be fringed on three sides. Sarah's hair may be drawn back and allowed to hang down in the rear. A twisted fillet of gold may be worn around the head, for this was one of the various styles of headdress. There were others, but they are less attractive to the modern mind and notion of what constitutes a becoming style.

Sarah also may wear sandals like those of Abraham. For ornaments, a dog collar and three- or four-inch arm bands just above the elbow might be worn. The dog collar may also imitate gold, upon which black geometric designs are painted. Long, dangling earrings complete the picture of a lady of high rank in Ur of the Chaldees.

* Crepe hair, as used on the stage, was originally made of real hair, later of silk. It comes wound around string. After cutting the string at one end, the hair unravels in a crinkly condition. The crepe hair then may be combed gently and cut to the desired length.

Figure 18—Abraham and Sarah in the Wilderness.

Abraham and Sarah in the Wilderness

When Abraham and Sarah went into the Wilderness, they donned more protective, voluminous garments. For these, the draped-sheet tunic may be used, over which should be worn the aba. Both Abraham and Sarah should wear the aba. However, there should be no stripes on this garment. (See Figure 18A.) The headdress of Abraham is the typical kerchief and tire as in Figure 9B. Sarah might wear a similar headdress with a white veil (starched cheesecloth or tobacco cloth) thrown over it, covering the throat and shoulders.

Isaac, Jacob and Esau

The boy Isaac should be simply clothed, wearing a sheepskin, or short tunic of burlap, draped over one shoulder. If the tunic is used, a narrow colorful girdle should be worn. The only material that in any way resembles sheepskin is bath-toweling dyed a dark ecru.

The garments of Jacob and Esau are equally quite simple. Although we have scant information concerning these characters, we know from the Bible that Jacob and Esau lived close to nature and could very easily have worn sheepskins, either hanging from the waistline or thrown over the left shoulder.

In lieu of sheepskins, for which there does not seem to be an adequate substitute, an imitation of the coarser woolen materials may be used. As stated earlier, burlap sacks give this impression. A soft garment should be worn next to the body, because burlap is quite irritating to the skin.

There is, however, at the present writing, a leopard-skin pattern which is very popular, being used for auto-seat covers, shirts, and even raincoats. If some of these articles have been discarded, their materials make excellent substitutes for leopard skin. It is conceivable that early Old Testament people did more than try to frighten wild animals from their flocks. Consequently, they wore the skins of slain wild beasts as well as the skins of the sheep that might have been used for food. A leopard skin is a good contrast with sheepskin. The animal skins may be girded with a cord.

Rachel, Rebecca

Rachel, Rebecca, Ruth and Naomi, Jephthah's daughter and other women of the Old Testament should be dressed a little differently from those of the New Testament. A sleeveless, striped tunic, with a narrow girdle one inch wide, is the most common costume. The tunic is the narrow, straight undergarment of Figure 1A. On this are basted rather wide dark stripes.

If more than the tunic is worn, the full striped aba should be used in preference to an overdrape. The tunic in this case should be girded with a wide and long-fringed sash. A stiff, white veil, like Sarah's, was also worn over the headdress, which would be the conventional Hebrew kerchief and tire. Should the story of Ruth be dramatized, Ruth and Naomi might don such garments on the journey back to Naomi's homeland. In fact, the two women could very well imitate the garb of Sarah in the Wilderness.

The Time of Joseph

Joseph and His Brothers

Before Joseph was sold into Egypt, the costumes of all the characters connected with his story should be of the conventional Hebrew type. That is, the tunic and aba. The sleeveless aba is in keeping with the time of Joseph because of its closer association with Abraham and the Wilderness than with any of the later periods.

According to the *Abingdon Bible Commentary* (see "References"), Joseph, although not the eldest, was Jacob's favorite son. Therefore, he wore a long-sleeved coat, indicating that he was to be a gentleman and consequently would be expected to do no work. The aba of Abraham may be used for the "coat of many colors," with the addition of three-inch stripes of yellow, wine red and dark green basted on the material. When Joseph's coat is taken from him, he should be wearing a tunic with a girdle. The girdle in this instance may be of cloth. One of the kerchiefs described under "The Headdress and the Girdle" in Section I is suggested.

The brothers, if all eleven are depicted, should wear corresponding tunics and abas, the abas not being as elaborate as Joseph's nor with so long a sleeve. Since they probably will not remove their outer garments, the draped-sheet or cotton-blanket tunics may be worn. However, unless there is enough money in the treasury, a play using this many male characters had best be studied from all angles first. Eleven draped sheets or blankets, even as undergarments, tend to look monotonous. A variety is needed, but not every group has funds to purchase material for eleven abas or eleven tunics.

The Slave Buyers

The fact that Joseph was sold in Egypt does not mean that the slave buyers were necessarily Egyptian. They easily could have been the roaming type, buying in one country and selling in another. So that they would be somewhat different in appearance, their headdresses might be more elaborate in character. On each head, two thick tires separated in front and brought together in the rear may be used, plus the kerchief large enough to be brought around in front, and draped so that it conceals the lower part of the face, as if for greater protection against the blowing sands of the des-

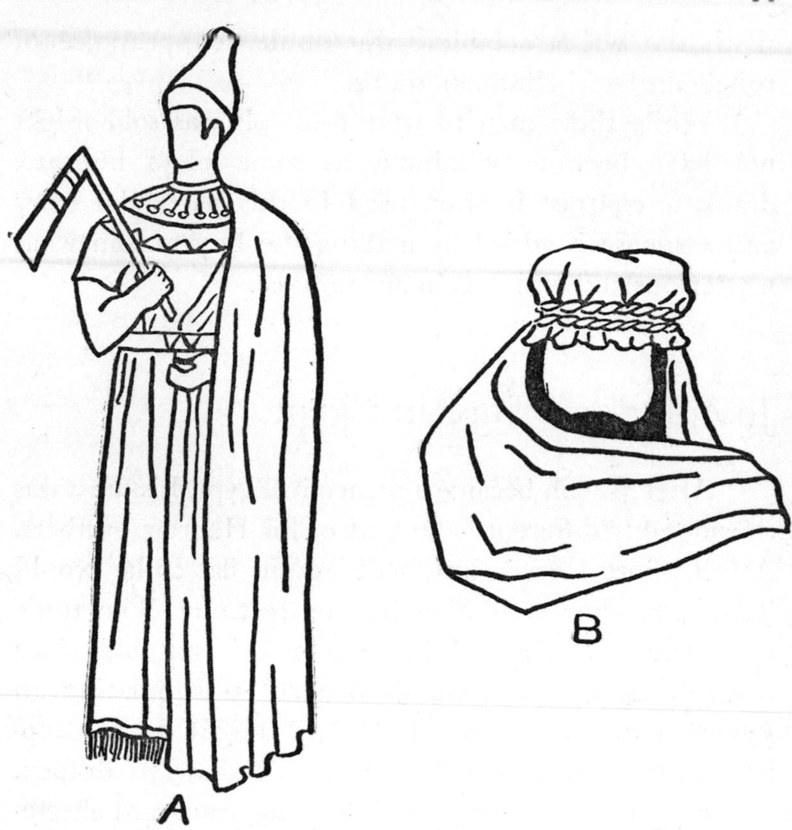

Figure 19—A: Joseph as a prince in Egypt. B: Headdress of slave buyer.

ert. (See Figure 19B.) One of the lighter-colored cheesecloth veils may be used for this, doubling the material.

Wide, impressive leather belts, through which six-inch knives may be thrust, are worn next to the tunics, which may again be draped sheets or colored cotton blankets, as suggested in Section I. Sleeveless abas that reach the wrists complete the opulent appearance of rough dealers in human traffic.

While these men to whom Joseph was sold might not have been as villainous as some plays indicate, dramatic contrast is often used in this particular story and suspense is added by making the buyers somewhat mysterious and ominous in appearance.

Joseph as a Prince in Egypt

After Joseph became a prince in Egypt, his dress was considerably different from that of his Hebrew brothers. A full, short-sleeved tunic with round flat collar would have been the foundation for his costume. The tunic of Figure 1C, described in Section I, is suitable, since the fullness of the tunic is needed in simulating an Egyptian undergarment. The tunic might be of deep-blue color over which a gold-colored shawl is draped.

For this shawl, use one of the long, four-yard cheesecloth overdrapes, a length falling over the left shoulder to the floor in front, the rest trailing down the back. Over tunic and shawl, tie a narrow belt at the waist. Bring the shawl up from the back and throw over the same shoulder toward the front. The belt keeps the shawl in place in the rear and allows the loose front folds to fall over the whole of the left arm, as in Figure 19A. A section of the first part of the shawl that is fastened by the belt should be visible in front. This is accomplished by pulling the under portion of the shawl on a diagonal line from the shoulder to the belt.

The collar on this costume is made from a circular piece of old sheeting. The collar fits the neck snugly and extends the width of the shoulders. On this, in geometric design, baste or glue strips of colored cellophane. The best colors are red, Nile green, powder blue and dark yellow. The cellophane will reflect light and give a luxurious appearance.

Joseph should have a crown. This might be almost conical in shape, the lower part coming well down over the head and fitting tightly. The crown may be made from an old stocking-cap that has a tuft on top. The tuft should be shaped with shears so that it resembles the small extension on the top of the crown. Most communities have at least one milliner who is willing to lend a head form for a day. Over this form, the heavily starched stocking-cap, while still wet, may be stretched, first padding the cap with soft cloths to attain the shape shown in Figure 19A. Be sure to cut out the eartabs first and pull down over the head form as far as possible. Allow the material to dry. The starch may cause the padding to adhere to the cap, so cut the padding away as much as possible without destroying the shape. After removing the crown from the form, cover with gold paint, which may be purchased at any ten-cent store. The addition of paint not only makes an imposing appearance for the crown, but adds greater stiffness.

To give Joseph higher prestige in the minds of his brothers, a guard might accompany him. For this character, a tunic or short skirt is needed, as well as armor of dressed leather from breast to waist, held in place by a two-inch strap over each shoulder. The armor may be made from flannelette and dyed dark brown. It is similar to the Roman armor described in Section I, except that it should look as though it were of one piece.

If Pharaoh is impersonated, he may be dressed as described in "The Time of Moses," where the Egyptian dress is discussed in greater detail.

The Time of Moses

The Egyptians again come into the picture in the story of Moses. This time the women, from the lowly to the exalted, play prominent parts. It might be well to start with the lowly since they wore a very simple dress.

The Mother and Sister of Moses

Because the Israelites had been taken in slavery to Egypt, the mother of Moses and his sister should be shown as humble Egyptians. The scant, sleeveless tunic to the ankles, with a narrow belt, constitutes the costume. A short necklace of shells might be worn to add a small touch of feminine loveliness.

The Egyptian Princess and Attendants

When Pharaoh's daughter and her handmaidens discovered the infant Moses in the bullrushes, the handmaidens probably wore a tunic with a full skirt, form-fitting in the back and full in the front. Much of the Egyptian dress seemed to reveal the figures of both men and women. Type 1C is used for this tunic. The handmaidens, to be distinguishable from the Hebrew slaves, might wear a flat circular collar with geometric designs. This collar should be narrower than that worn by the princess, whose collar should be quite elaborately embroidered with bright thread and precious stones.

The princess herself should wear a tunic quite full in the front, form-fitting in the rear. Again type 1C is suggested for this. The girdle should be rather long and about one inch wide, first being placed high-waisted and tied in back, securely held in place with a safety pin inconspicuously used. It is then brought down around the hips and tied in front, hanging almost to the hem of the tunic, which is ankle length.

Over the shoulders of the princess and reaching to her elbows is placed a rectangular piece of cloth, the mantle, the ends of which are brought together in the center of the chest and fastened with a clasp. Here again one of the cheesecloth overdrapes may be used. This time, however, it should be white, since the persons of royalty and higher rank wore white linen of beautifully sheer quality. Fold the four-yard length of

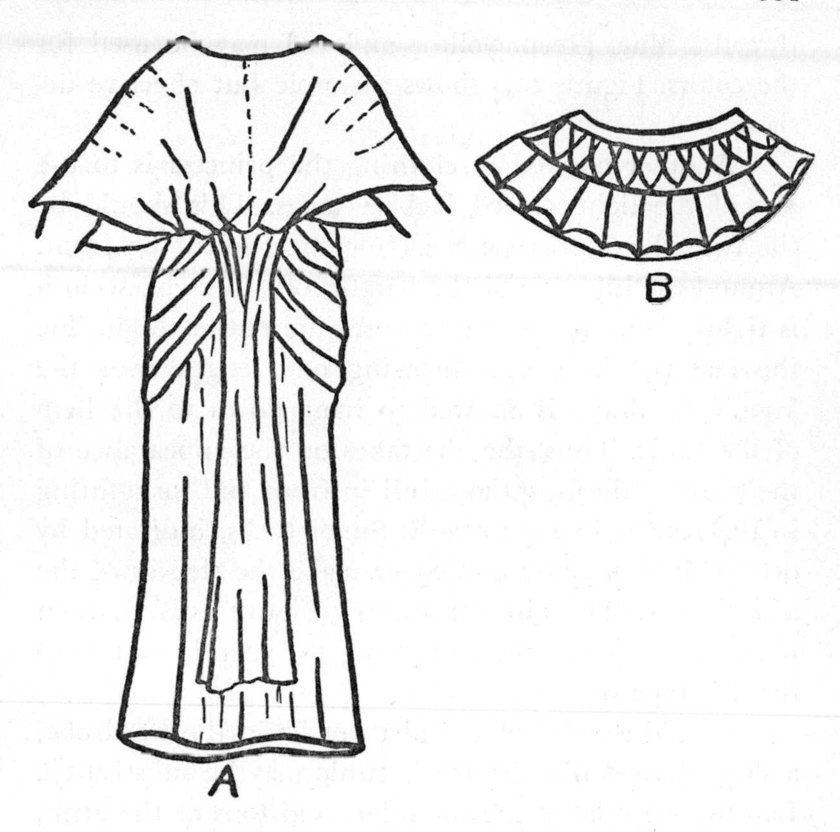

Figure 20—A: Aba and drape arranged for Egyptian princess. B: Design for Egyptian collar.

cheesecloth or tobacco cloth until it fits the wearer. These several layers will have a tendency to shimmer, which is perfectly all right.

Over this mantle place the flat, round collar that is mentioned in "The Time of Joseph," and under "Accessories" in Section I. The collar should give the appearance of being embroidered with colored stones and threads. Blue, green, yellow and red may be used for the colors. Figure 20B shows a simple but effective design.

Another method of clothing the princess is to use one of the light-colored Hebrew abas. This should be the full, sleeveless type sewn together down the front. Around the hips one of the lengths of white cheesecloth is tightly bound so that it encases the entire thigh. Tie the material in front, throwing one length over the knot. The drape is allowed to hang down to the hem of the tunic. Thus, the aba takes on the appearance of the tunic of the Egyptians, full in front and form-fitting in the rear as in Figure 20A. Small tucks, indicated by dotted lines, may be needed to make the sleeves of the aba shorter. The circular collar (Figure 20B) is then placed around the neck, omitting the mantle and clasp for this type of tunic.

Should a light-colored aba not be in the wardrobe, a sheet draped like the Doric tunic may be substituted. Lap the material at the shoulders and tops of the arms, front over back, and secure underneath with small pins. In using either the aba or the sheet, the arms should be held shoulder high while the cheesecloth drape is arranged around the hips. Over the sheet-tunic the Egyptian collar again takes its place.

On her forearms the princess may wear several two-inch bands fastened together with a narrow vertical band. The princess in this story probably wore a wig and fillet.

Should the wig evoke laughter among the cast, it is possible that the audience will react in a similar manner. So it is better to omit the wig and let the princess wear a fillet around her own loose hair. In the center of the forehead and attached to the fillet, a lotus blossom may be worn. This was the custom of Egyptian women, who sometimes wore the blossom on the top of the head. Even if the wig is worn, the princess should wear the fillet and lotus blossom.

One of the characteristics of Egyptian dress is the radiation point. That is, there is a point on the dress from which the lines seem to radiate. For instance, the clasp in the center of the mantle (the rectangular piece of cloth worn over the shoulders) seems to be the point of radiation, and the center of the girdle in front appears to be the point from which the folds of the skirt for both men and women radiate.

The drcss of thc men appearing in the story of Moses was most simple. Because the climate was hot, they wore little clothing. A short skirt, similar in appearance to the mantle described for the princess, was draped about the loins and secured with a girdle. A triangular tab or apron depended from the center with the point at the girdle. The elaborateness of this apron depicted the rank of the wearer. The king wore a very beautifully embroidered and jeweled apron of many colors. Sometimes enamel was used.

It is possible that some parish and school communities will disapprove of the authentic Egyptian costume for the men, even though the members of the cast possess strong and athletic-looking physiques. The following adaptations may be made to meet such objections.

Tunics of sheer linen were sometimes worn either under or over the skirt and apron of the men. Since this was the case, a white tunic of nontransparent cloth may be worn next to the skin, letting the draped skirt and apron carry the impression that the person is an Egyptian. With a rounded, flat collar, girdle, headdress, and sandals turned up at the toes, the person is adequately clothed for a church or school audience and yet authentic enough to look Egyptian. Pharaoh and Joseph might be dressed thus, with very elaborate accessories. The inverted "V"-shaped apron depending from the belt should have bright-colored designs emblazoned on it. The collar, as has been stated, should be most elaborate as though precious stones were embedded in the material. Colored cellophane may be used for this effect.

Some authorities indeed show Joseph in this manner of dress. His headdress, then, should be like that pictured in Figure 10B. Pharaoh should wear many jeweled arm bands on fore and upper arms. His headdress may be similar to that of Joseph's as a prince (Figure 19A), with a colored or jeweled visorlike piece of two-inch width in front.

The Time of David

The Assyrian influence on dress was apparent during the time of David. Tissot's painting, *The Friendship of David and Jonathan,* shows Jonathan and his warriors in armor, with fringed tunics draped in typical Assyrian fashion. David himself, without armor, wears the fringed tunic. Again, Tissot pictures David donning the armor of Saul, and the fringed garments are much in evidence.

Young David

David, as a shepherd lad, needs little more than an animal skin over his left shoulder and around his body. This might be either the leopard skin (page 91), or a throw of burlap material as described on page 35. As a young man, he probably wore clothes of Assyrian character. The fringed shawl draped in skirtlike manner from the waist to the knees gave freedom of movement, and the torso and arms would have been covered by a tunic. The wide, two-piece Assyrian belt completed the outfit.

King David

As king, David probably wore over his long, fringed tunic the typical Assyrian shawl shown in Figure 6A.

The artist Lilien shows an attractive headdress in his sketch of David as king. Two twenty-four-inch pieces of white cheesecloth may be used for this. The first piece is placed off-center over the head so that the longer right end may be thrown loosely across the lower part of the throat and over the left shoulder. The second piece is bound rather loosely around the head in the usual Hebrew fashion, the ends hanging down the back. Across the front of the turban, over the brows, is a single row of pearls, stretching from temple to temple. Centered on the front of the turban is the traditional six-point Star of David outlined in jewels, on either side of which is a large, round jewel, possibly amethyst. The pearls continue from the temples to the round jewels, which appear to be connected to the Star of David by several more pearls. A long double strand of pearls is draped from temple to temple, necklacelike, so that it more or less forms an outline for the loose drapery across the throat.

To help this gracefully folded headdress stay more securely in place, a felt skullcap may be used as foundation. To this, the material may be either pinned or basted.

Instead of the bushy, square Assyrian beard, Lilien gives his David a short, double Vandyke beard, and a narrow mustache. The double Vandyke is not clean-cut but tapers off into a sketchy beard.

Saul and Jonathan

Saul and Jonathan should be dressed as Assyrian king and nobleman, respectively. Their outfits consist of the usual fringed tunic, over which is draped the large fringed shawl. The simple arrangement of the Assyrian shawl, as described in Section I under "The Cloak and the Overdrape," is sufficient. The Assyrian headdress for kings, also described in Section I under "The Headdress," should be used for Saul and Jonathan. The Assyrian beard, made of black crepe hair, gives the austerity noted in Assyrian characters. Saul might also carry the mace, which was a twenty-four-inch stick with a decorated knob.

Authorities are consistent in their discussions concerning the ornateness of dress in regard to the Assyrian-Babylonian period. Very seldom were plain materials used, decorations of all kinds being lavishly woven into the cloth or painted thereon. Bracelets, arm bands, heavy earrings, necklaces, dog collars and anklets were worn, especially by the men. The body, plainly clothed, would not strike terror into the hearts of lesser people nearly as much as a heavily bedecked body and a head and face covered with black bushy hair and beard. The Assyrians were noted for their cruelty and were more warlike than any other nation in the Old Testament.

For general stage purposes, however, the tunics and shawls need not be decorated except for the heavy fringe. The other accessories may be worn as lavishly as desired, which will enhance the general appearance of barbarity. A knife or two thrust into the two-piece Assyrian belt, a sword hung from a leather strap which crosses the body from right shoulder to left hip, add greatly to the effect of military aggressiveness.

The Time of Esther

The story of Esther has dramatic high spots of suspense and rare beauty. The types of characters are varied, ranging from the heroine who possesses bravery as well as beauty, to the villain who, according to Old Testament standards, meets the end that is due him. Intrigue and jealousy receive their own deserved fate, as courage and loyalty win their rewards. It is a story that should capture the imagination of those seeking romance and adventure.

When we costume these characters, we must study the Persians. Like the Assyrians, the Persians employed the tunic and shawl. More often, however, the robe was used instead of the shawl.

Esther, the Girl

Esther, although living in a foreign land, was still a Hebrew maid. Her clothes, therefore, at the beginning of the story, would have been Hebrew. For stage use, the sleeveless, striped tunic, girded with a narrow ribbon are sufficient. She might, when she first appears before King Ahasuerus, wear a headdress composed of a long, white veil upon which tiers of spangles are placed to hold the veil upon the head. Simple sandals complete the outfit.

Esther, the Queen

Her costume as the queen should have, in addition to the foregoing dress, a small embroidered collar over which a gold necklace is placed. There are no Hebrew stripes on the tunic, however, but fringe should be added on the hem. The short-sleeved tunic of Figure 1C may be used for this. A Persian scarf, twelve inches wide and three yards long, with fringe on one long side and both ends, is draped in the following manner. Over the right shoulder, with the plain edge toward the neck, drop the scarf almost to the knee in front. Bring the rest around the neck in back, over the left shoulder and to the right hip or breast. Continue the scarf around in back, reversing it so that the fringe is turned *in* under the left arm to the front and throw over the left shoulder

Figure 21—King Ahasuerus and Queen Esther.

so that the remainder of the scarf hangs down the back, as in Figure 21B.

One of the brighter-blue cheesecloth overdrapes, with dark-blue fringe added, may be used for this scarf. The overdrape may be three feet wide but should be in double thickness before the fringe is added. The double-thick shawl will appear more luxurious, and so more suitable for the queen.

Mordecai, the Uncle

In order to have contrast in the costume of Esther's uncle, Mordecai, he might appear typically Hebrew in the first scenes with a tunic, aba, and headdress of the usual kerchief and tire. When he is honored by the king, he may wear, instead of the aba, a shawl draped in the simple manner suggested in Section I, under "Assyrian" in "The Cloak and the Overdrape." Mordecai's headdress at this stage of his life might imitate the king's crown as described in the second paragraph following. Instead of the knobs, tips of feathers may be substituted. The headdress should not be as elaborate in design as that of the king's crown.

Ahasuerus, the King

King Ahasuerus is not too difficult to dress. A Hebrew aba like that in Figure 4A, without stripes, may be girded with a large cordlike belt (two kerchiefs rolled and twisted) drawing up the sides so that they are somewhat shorter than the front and back. The girdle will help form the sleeves, which should be very full. The aba may or may not be basted together in front; if not, a tunic should be worn. Since all basic tunics and cloaks should have deep hems, the hem on this aba should be let out to allow for easier draping of the sleeves and still keep the garment long. Although some of the tunics were in figured cloth, plain colors will do as well. To relieve the plainness, two narrow stripes about two inches apart may be added on the hems of the skirt and sleeves.

The king should wear a crown of gold at least six inches in height. The top circumference of the crown is somewhat larger than the bottom. The top rim may be uneven, with small round knobs. The crown may be decorated with indistinct and dissimilar figures. Use the pattern shown in Figure 11B (turban of the Assyrian male) for making the king's crown, but use it inverted. The top should be left open. On the king's feet are cloth shoes with straps over the instep. Heavy woolen socks, dyed brown, may be used for these with darker brown strips of cloth sewn over the instep to give the appearance of half-inch straps. A long, straight staff, five and one-half feet in length, topped with an uneven gold knob, adds to his regalia. Earrings were worn by men in general, and King Ahasuerus might wear heavy drop earrings. A pointed black beard, made of unkinked crepe hair and extending to the breastbone, should be worn by the king and the villain, Haman, alike. Crepe hair may be used for the bushy black hair to cover the back of the neck. The crepe hair may be fastened with spirit gum to the inside of the crown or headdress. Seldom are headdresses of Biblical times removed in sight of an audience, hence the expedient method of joining the crepe hair and headdress.

Haman, the Villain

Over a straight tunic, Haman might wear a Persian robe similar to the Hebrew aba, except for long and narrower sleeves and a three-inch flat collar—square corners in the back and front—extending a little below the armpit in front. Ties similar to shoestrings are fastened at the corners of the collar. Haman's headdress should appear in style similar to the one described for Mordecai after being honored by the King.

Vashti, the Deposed Queen

If Vashti, the deposed queen, is characterized, she may dress similarly to Queen Esther, but possibly more ornately decorated with bracelets and necklaces. Any serving maid who might accompany her would be Hebrew and costumed similar to Esther before she became queen, without any headdress, however.

The Time of the Prophets

In preparing costumes for the prophets of the Old Testament, we should particularly strive for a nonspecific effect as to time and place. To the members of an average audience, they are shadowy and somewhat unreal personages. Nevertheless, they did live and should at least convey this impression to the audience. The false prophets, of which there were many, prophesied for personal prestige and material gain, and were prone to tell the people what they wished to hear. On the other hand, the true prophets, like Elisha, Elijah, Isaiah and Jeremiah, tried to make the people realize that continuation of their sinful ways would lead to destruction. They were men of great heart and understanding who lived close to their God.

With this observation in mind, the men of God

should appear like the great characters they were, unruffled by the taunts and jibes of the people they tried to warn. This can be done if the tone and color in dress of the prophets are in marked contrast to the garments of the people. A somber note should be predominant in the coloring of the dress of the prophets, especially if these men are depicted in contrast to a giddy and unmindful populace. This is true in the oratorio, *Elijah,* where the jeering mob should be clothed in bright and even garish colors. The earthiness of the Priests of Baal is outstanding in the flashy garments. Elijah, on the other hand, should be costumed in dull tones, probably wearing a dark full tunic, over which an aba of the sleeveless variety may be used. To relieve the austerity of the costume, however, a cloth girdle of lighter color might be worn over the tunic. Dark, wide stripes of contrasting color, basted on the aba, will have a tendency to enlarge the figure. Voluminous garments are in keeping with the character of the prophets.

The headdress of any of the prophets is the usual Hebrew kerchief and tire, the kerchief being somewhat larger than ordinary. The tire, too, may be thick, as differentiated from the ropelike ones often worn. A double tire such as shown in Figure 9C is in keeping with the character.

Section Three

The Time of the Nativity

To differentiate the women of the New Testament from those of the Old, the shawl draped somewhat like the Greek himation should be worn more often than the aba. The sheet foundation, whether white or pastel, may still be used for a good many of the female characters because the overdrapes are arranged to cover the greater part of the foundation.

The Virgin Mary

Blue, the traditional color for purity, is very often used for the overdrape of the Virgin Mary. No shade is quite as lovely as powder blue draped in the manner shown in Figure 7. Powder blue is the color of a blue sky on a perfectly clear day. If a regular tunic is worn instead of a sheet, the overdrape often is thrown over the head in the usual manner, but is brought up in close soft folds around the throat and shoulders, rather than under one arm and across the front. This arrangement should not be used with a sheet foundation, however, since it covers only the shoulders, part of the arms and back.

A colored tunic of very light pink makes a simple but lovely combination with the powder-blue drape. The light pink and this shade of blue make one think of sunrise. Frequently, no girdle is worn.

The Angels

If the Angel of the Annunciation is used, simple, flowing lines are needed. White rayon gives a shimmering, ethereal effect. A straight full tunic, gathered around the neck, with long sleeves of the aba-type, constitutes practically the entire costume.

No wings? Yes, no wings. In order to make wings large enough in proportion to an adult body, much painstaking effort is needed, and the results are seldom adequate. The only time the author witnessed a production where wings on an angel added greatly to the majesty and awesomeness of the picture was in a dramatic presentation of the oratorio *Elijah*. The Angel appeared in the large opening of the baptistry, which was high above the heads of the choir tiered above the platform. With the playing area on the stage darkened, and a blue spot focused on the Angel, a feeling of awe and grandeur was created. The wings were huge and graceful, and the distance from the audience helped create the illusion of an ethereal being. The poor Angel, however, could not sit down off-stage during the production because her wings would not permit her to. And these additions to her body were far from comfortable since they were on a harness strapped tightly to her back, yet not too tightly because the Angel had to sing! Nevertheless, the effect was breathtaking not only for the Angel but for the audience.

However, for the average school and church production where the players are close to the audience and the lighting is not too adequate, it is well to dispense with angel wings per se and to dwell on perfecting an impression. If Gabriel practices rising on tiptoes slowly and at the same time raises his hands until they are over his head, arm length with the elbows slightly bent, the audience will almost see wings unfolding, especially if the long sleeves are triangular in shape with the long side hanging from the wrists. The effect is greatly enhanced if the lights are cut at the peak of the action. If not, a slow backward withdrawal, maintaining the poised-to-flight position, is thoroughly adequate.

Also, omit any Christmas tree tinsel that you may have the urge to use. It adds nothing but a tawdry glitter, quite unethereal in appearance. The simple, shimmering gown is entirely sufficient.

If rayon is too expensive, a good grade of white cheesecloth makes an adequate substitute. Be sure there is a white, ankle-length garment under it. Since cheesecloth has a tendency to cling, it is advisable to put weights in the lower point of the triangular sleeve.

If Gabriel is impersonated by a man, a halo may be omitted. However, if a girl takes the part, a halo adds greatly to the effect. This is made from suit-box cardboard. It is like the brim of a hat, about five or six inches wide. There is no crown, nothing but a hole cut to fit the wearer when the halo is placed on the back of the head. The halo is more interesting if made in the shape of an ellipse with the hole sufficiently off-center to allow freedom in turning the head. In other words, the hole is nearer the neck-end of the ellipse. The cardboard is covered with aluminum paint, or aluminum relieved with three black stripes about two inches wide at the hole, and radiating like the rays of the sun to three inches, one stripe on each side and the third at the center. The hair should be loose but not enough to cover the face in profile.

Mary and Joseph

When we come to costuming the Nativity scene we consider Mary, Joseph, the shepherds and Wise Men, the Heavenly Host, the innkeeper and possible members of his family, and the soldiers of Herod.

The blue overdrape still may be used for Mary, and quite often is preferred, although other pastel shades are equally suitable. Light green, or a combination of light green with a darker green, or even powder blue and a lining of orange or yellow, change the tone of the picture.

Joseph usually wears the traditional headdress, tunic and aba. If not the aba, a double thickness of navy-blue or dark-brown cheesecloth to simulate the heavy shawl thrown over one shoulder, as in Figure 8A, is suitable. The headdress should be somewhat in contrast to the aba, or drape. That is, the somber shades are reserved for the larger pieces of material on the men, but the headdresses or girdles, in order to relieve the dullness, may be brighter.

Should Joseph wear a navy-blue drape, the kerchief might be yellow with inch-wide stripes of navy blue basted on the material. The stripes are about two inches apart so that the yellow is predominant. The tire may be of two colors, navy blue and dark yellow twisted together, as in Figure 9B, or a double tire as shown in Figure 9C.

Joseph might wear a plain, dark-brown aba or brown relieved by two-inch stripes of dark red or dark yellow basted on the material. With this kind of aba, a yellow or dark-yellow headdress with dark-red tire may be used.

An admonition is necessary at this point. So often those in charge of costumes make the mistake of overplaying certain combinations of colors on the same costume. For instance, a woman might be wearing a yellow tunic. Her long headdress, as in Figure 7, is light green, the tire is yellow and her girdle green and yellow. The sin of monotony is committed here. It may be relieved by putting on either a girdle or a tire of navy blue. The sharp contrast keeps the picture from slipping into the distance. Some of us who have been in the production end for many years quite often say, "When in doubt, use navy blue." It is a neutral color for costumes, just as neutral gray is for staging. Of course, even this can be overdone, but discretion is always an admirable trait to acquire.

The Innkeeper and His Family

The innkeeper may be prosperous or not, according to the script. If prosperous, his cloak, over the sheet foundation, may be that of the Old Testament Joseph with the stripes removed. Flannel dyed a dark brown is somber but rich-looking. The headdress may be purple with a gold-colored tire. A gold girdle, or one of imitation leather with colored-cellophane "stones," completes his ensemble.

His wife may wear a dark-yellow tunic and either a medium shade of green or orchid overdrape.

Perhaps the innkeeper has a daughter. She may be dressed in style similar to the mother's, but in light pastel shades. There might be bright embroidery around the neck of the tunic. (See description of embroidery under "Accessories" in Section I.)

If there is a maidservant, she should wear a tunic in contrast to the yellow. Whatever the color of the drape the wife uses, make sure that the tunic on the maidservant is not the same. The headdress is a single veil about waist length with contrasting narrow tire. The girdle may be any dark shade.

The Shepherds

Since the men who did the actual shepherding of the flocks seldom were too prosperous, their dress would tend toward the rougher materials, that of homespun. Knee-length tunics of burlap will help give the effect of sturdiness. To keep the burlap from maintaining its sacklike appearance, dark girdles should be worn. The younger shepherds and shepherd boys might be clothed in such attire. They frequently went bareheaded. The adult shepherds should wear ankle-length tunics, and headdresses.

Often the "green pastures" were some distance from the fold and the shepherds would stay out in the hills for days at a time. Palestinian nights were chilly, sometimes cold, so more than the tunic was needed. Abas, then, were protection against the elements. In the Nativity scene, the shepherds "were watching their flocks by night." In this case, abas should be added. These abas could very well be made of the burlap sacks, the men wearing the conventional-length abas, the boys knee-length.

The Wise Men

The Wise Men are often depicted as coming from three different countries. Sometimes they represent three different races. Whatever the interpretation, it is better to make them indefinite, following the suggestion in the Introduction. Indefinite but different. Yet they should give the impression that they are men of great importance, very possibly of a priestly order.

All Three Wise Men may wear sheetlike tunics if they wear cloaks or heavy drapes of dark and rich colors. One outergarment might be wine or dark red, another navy blue, and the third a dark green. It is better not to have stripes on the cloaks. If one Wise Man wears drapes, the material should be twice as wide as that worn by the Hebrew people. That means four lengths of the colored drapes should be used instead of two, using the double thickness. This heavy-appearing drape may be thrown over both shoulders from the front, the material being pulled low on the chest and the folds being allowed to fall gracefully over the arms, as in Figure 22C. This is an especially attractive arrangement of the overdrape, not belonging to any definite period or country. If this Wise Man wears a dark tunic, a gold-yellow overdrape will add a most luxurious touch.

Another way of draping one of the Wise Men is similar to that of the chlamys worn by Greek men. Put together two lengths of the dark cheesecloth and drape under the right arm, catching the rest of the material on the left shoulder with a large, impressive clasp. This will allow the ends of the material to hang in voluminous folds down front and back. The Wise Men as a rule do not have much more action than walking and kneeling, and these two types of drapes will add much to the luxurious and majestic appearance of these personages.

If a large-sleeved tunic is available, one of the Wise Men may do without a cloak or overdrape. A wide, ornate belt, described later, helps create the illusion of grandeur and adds variation to the picture.

There is always the problem of feet becoming entangled in long robes when a character rises from a kneeling position. This entanglement can be avoided if any character wearing voluminous clothing remembers that, upon kneeling, the feet are kept in exact position and not moved an inch. Upon rising, the feet are not moved until the position is erect. This, of course, takes practice many times before production night.

For head coverings, there should be crown effects. Two such crowns may be made with cardboard foundations of different shapes, as shown in Figure 22, inserts 1 and 2. The third, for variation, is composed of heavy padding fastened with safety pins over a skullcap which should fit the head snugly. Over the foundations are thrown long single thicknesses of very light yellow cheesecloth, in such a way as to maintain the shape of the crown. These veils give the mystic touch to the Magi, and should hang down the back almost touching the floor. (See Figures 22A, 22B and 22C.) The Wise Men in Figures 22A and 22B wear one length of the veil over a shoulder for illustrative purposes. On the front of the headdress may be placed gold or silver

Figure 22—The Three Wise Men, and patterns for crowns.

crescents. To make the crescents stand out, brush a little spirit gum (the liquid used for holding whiskers in place in make-up) on them, and while they are still wet, sprinkle a little Christmas snow. It will be just enough to catch whatever light is used. Sometimes around the headdress large tires are placed to add contrast to one or two of the Wise Men.

The Wise Men are often referred to as "kings." To help carry out this impression, wide leather belts decorated with colored stones may be used in place of cloth girdles. These are made as suggested in Section I under "The Girdle." However, if the Wise Men are elected to come from different countries or to be of different races, it is better to vary the type of girdles. One might wear the leather belt with precious stones, as in Figure 22B; another a two-toned cloth girdle twisted in soft folds; while the third might use a wide cloth girdle of gold color, or a girdle of cardboard painted gold-yellow to simulate gold. These belts will probably not show on the two Wise Men who may be wearing drapes but will help give the characters a feeling of opulence as befits kings.

The Heavenly Host

Should the Heavenly Host be seen as well as heard, costumes similar to that described for the Angel of the Annunciation would be thoroughly adequate. Halos may or may not be worn. If the Heavenly Host is an adult choir, halos should be omitted. A halo of any kind looks effeminate, and for a robust member of the bass section to wear one creates a picture of incongruity. Uniformity is usually the keynote as to appearance of a choir, so omit the halos from the heads of the ladies as well. On the other hand, if children up to ten or eleven years of age constitute the members of the choir, halos are attractive on boys as well as on girls.

The Soldiers of Herod

Because an atmosphere of beauty and hope is usually desired for the Nativity scene, the Roman soldier is not often used. But there are a few one-act plays that include him in the cast. If he is portrayed, he should be clothed in Roman armor as described in Section I. Full regalia makes him impressive. A large, scarlet mantle, worn much in the same manner as the Greek chlamys, but with the material on the right side thrown back over the shoulder, adds to his impressiveness, should the soldier carry the rank of centurion.

Jesus In His Ministry

The Hebrew people of the New Testament appear in a greater variety of clothing than do those of the Old Testament. They were now subservient to Rome. The mode of dress of Rome was influenced by that of Greece, which in turn was influenced by the powers preceding her.

The shawl or overdrape with its various arrangements was still popular and some of the Hebrew people adopted it. Others adhered to the traditional aba for the outer garment. This was true of the shepherds, and those traveling any distance from home. Also, a shorter cloak was worn by some merchants. The ecclesiastical order naturally was not influenced by the dress of those in power because its garments were prescribed by religious law.

Jesus

The figure of Jesus is not often seen in drama presentations by amateur casts. In most instances this is wise because of the difficulty of completely transforming any one into the likeness of the mental picture each of us has of Him. However, there are instances when large casts are used on appropriately large stages where the figure of Jesus might be observed at some distance from the audience. In such cases the entire scene would be of sufficient magnitude to depict the character of Jesus more as an influence than as an individual. The garments used would then depend upon where the emphasis of personality was placed. If Jesus is being portrayed in the role of The Good Shepherd, He might easily be presented in tunic and aba, as observed in paintings of The Good Shepherd. Should Jesus as The Teacher be emphasized, the tunic and overdrape are appropriate. In either case, the tunic should be white, and of the large-sleeved type of Figure 1B. If the aba is worn, it might be wine-colored and without stripes. Should the overdrape be preferred, wine again might be the color, purple, or even the lovely powder blue, depending upon the temper of the scene. A girdle of navy blue might be worn in any instance. As for the headdress, few if any of the paintings show Jesus with a head covering. A wig then is needed. This, of course, should be as flattering as possible. Again, interpretation of the character designates whether a blond wig or a brunet one is appropriate. The author is of the opinion that the brunet gives a stronger appearance for stage purposes. The figure may appear without sandals if desired, or sandals as in Figure 14B may be worn.

The Disciples

The Twelve Disciples represent several walks of life, giving us sufficient variety of dress.

Matthew might wear a sheet foundation with a leather girdle studded with a few stones. Being a tax collector, he should have a money bag and possibly a knife placed in the girdle. Over his tunic is a short cloak that reaches about to the knees. The color of this might be a plain, dark wine-red. The sleeves should be wide and flowing. The kerchief of the headdress could be the same color as the cloak, with a couple of one-inch stripes of navy blue on the end that hangs down the back. The tire could be yellow for contrast or twisted with navy blue. He wears sandals.

Costume Thomas in a light-yellow tunic with navy-blue shawl, as in Figure 9A, with a girdle of dark-green cloth like his headdress. The tire, as in Figure 9C, should have double coils of ochre. The tunic should be like that of Figure 1B.

Peter is usually depicted as a rugged fisherman, large in stature. In fact, everything that we know of him seems to be on a large scale, his fears, doubts, loyalty and love. So his costume should be generous. The tunic might be of brown or gray—the cotton blanket will add greatly to the player's physique in case it is necessary to dress a slight figure. A girdle of ochre is good contrast. The overdrape might be of wine-red or red-ochre. Since he is a fisherman, he might wear an aba, but the voluminous folds of a drape or shawl would be better.

If the cut of the hair is not too modern, no headdress is needed. However, Peter usually wears a beard and beards are difficult to match with the hair as well as to connect with the hairline. Too often the beard looks "stuck on." So a headdress would be necessary. A light-gray kerchief with navy-blue tire completes the costume.

Not often are the Twelve Disciples depicted together on the amateur stage except in the famous picture of *The Last Supper,* which some churches are using in their communion services on Good Friday. Usually it is too difficult to find twelve men in one locality who will submit to beards and flowing robes if they have to do more than just sit and look the part. But if a group is fortunate enough to possess this many male characters, the chart opposite should help give an idea of how to dress the Twelve. It is merely a suggestion to indicate the various color combinations and variety of dress. These outfits may be used for other Hebrew characters in the New Testament.

The Levite

The apparel of the Levite, or under-priest, was quite simple. A long-sleeved, close-fitting tunic is sufficient to

Chart For The Twelve Disciples

CHARACTER	TUNIC	ABA OF OVERDRAPE	HEADDRESS
PETER	brown or gray	wine-red or red-ochre overdrape	light gray with navy-blue tire
JAMES	sheet	old-rose overdrape	purple with yellow tire
JOHN	light green	dark-orange overdrape	ochre-yellow with gray tire
ANDREW	sheet	dark gray with wine and yellow stripes (aba)	navy blue with yellow tire
MATTHEW	sheet	dark-wine-red short aba	wine and navy-blue stripes with yellow tire or yellow and navy blue (twisted)
THOMAS	light yellow	navy-blue overdrape	dark green with double ochre tire
JUDAS	old rose	purple overdrape	no headdress, or yellow or navy-blue tire
JAMES (The Other)	dark blue	wine and yellow stripes (aba)	dark green with dark-yellow tire
SIMON	dark green	light-yellow overdrape	navy blue with dark-yellow tire
BARTHOLOMEW	light yellow	brown with navy-blue wide stripes (aba)	red-ochre with orchid tire
THADDEUS	ochre	red-ochre overdrape	yellow-ochre with purple tire
PHILIP	gray	plain navy-blue aba	powder blue with wine-red tire

suggest the difference between him and other ecclesiastical characters. In order to achieve this effect, the sleeveless tunic of Figure 1A is suggested. The tight-fitting wrist-length sleeves may be basted in, or snaps may be used around the armholes. Since these long sleeves are also used in the dress of the Roman woman, it is well to keep a pair or two of them on hand.

The tunic was girded with a ribbon seven or eight yards in length and three inches in width. Old sheeting may be used for this and embroidered in the ritual colors of blue, purple and scarlet. A design of small rectangles, end to end on the length of the ribbon, will be quite authentic. Colored crayon may be used to attain the effect of embroidery, breaking the lines so that the rectangles are never completely outlined.

The girdle is put on in the following manner: Starting with the center of the ribbon at the nape of the neck, pull the ribbon down at this point to about three or four inches above the natural waistline. Throw the ends over the shoulders to the front, forming a "V," and carry around to the back and pass through the point of the "V" which was pulled down in back. Wrap the ribbon around the body three more times, each row below the previous one, knot and loop each time in front, and the last two times cross at the waistline in back. The remaining ends hang almost to the hem of the tunic in front as in Figure 23C.

To complete the costume, a white linen cap is worn, This may be made by using a kerchief over padding fastened to a skullcap. Around the lower rim a wide tire is placed. The cap fits to the ears. Shoulder-length hair should be worn in the rear, similar to that suggested for Abraham in Section II.

The High Priest

The High Priest was more elaborately dressed. Over the tunic was a narrow robe, deep blue in color, which reached to the knees. It was hemmed at the bottom and decorated with pomegranates in pairs and embroidered in the ritual colors of blue, purple and scarlet. Between each pair of pomegranates was a small golden bell. These bells were real and made a tinkling sound when the High Priest walked.

For this robe, two lengths of the shorter cheesecloth overdrapes may be brought into use. Each piece being double, baste together the folded ends, leaving enough space for the head. Then baste together the lengths at each side, allowing for armholes. Probably the material will be too long for the knee-length robe, so turn it up and baste for the desired length. Make the pomegranates of old sheeting, color with show-card paint and tack on the hem. Bells need not be added for the general effect, but they aid in making the appearance more authentic. Small, flat bells cut from thin cardboard and fastened by the stem help give the illusion that the bells are real, especially if small, round bells from the ten-cent store are secured in the right places on the underneath side of the robe.

Over this robe was worn the "ephod," which was something like an apron. Again old sheeting may be used, making two rectangles thirty by ten inches, and fastened together at the shoulders by shoulder straps about ten inches in length. The ephod may be fringed on the ends. Arrange the girdle like that of the Levite.

The "breastplate of judgment" may be made of thin cardboard, four and one-half inches by eight, and attached to the shoulder straps lengthwise across the chest. On this paste twelve rosettes of cellophane to resemble the jewels which in the original represented the twelve tribes of Israel. These should be arranged in three rows, four jewels to a row. According to Moffat's translation of the New Testament, the first row consisted of jasper (yellow), chrysolite (olive-green), and crystal (clear); the second row, garnet (deep red), sapphire (deep blue), and sardonyx (reddish); the third row, cairngorm (brown), agate (moss-green) and amethyst (purple); and the last row, topaz (yellow), beryl (emerald-green, light blue or yellow) and onyx (black). Some of these colors, especially black, brown and the different shades of green, may be difficult to find in the cellophane. If the rosettes of cellophane are flat enough, the jewels for which colored cellophane can not be purchased, may be daubed on with thick show-card paint, making the paint stand up. By experimenting with small quantities of paint, the desired color may be secured. Over these daubs of paint may be glued small pieces of clear cellophane. The cellophane may be omitted but it does lend a sparkle to this kind of flat paint. In fact, cellophane may be omitted entirely and show-card paint substituted. The jewels will not only be more uniform in appearance, but it will be easier to make the color of the jewels more like the original.

Although the breastplate was attached to the ephod by loops of gold and small links of chain, this need not be the case for stage purposes. The four corners may be sewed to the ephod and blue cord attached to give the impression that the cord is the means of attachment.

The "miter" or headdress of the High Priest in some instances was similar to that of the Levite. It was, however, higher, and blue in color, worn over the white turban of the Levite. A variation of this, and one which is familiar to most audiences, is pictured in Figure 23A. Figure 23B shows the patterns for making this type of miter. Cardboard of the kind used for posters is suggested because it is heavier than suit-box grade. The author has kept all the discarded posters that the church displayed and has found many occasions for their use. The reverse side seldom has printing of any kind and makes excellent foundations. The miter may be made as follows, the dimensions given being for an average head size.

Using a radius of six and one-half inches, make a semicircle, *a,* in pattern No. 1. Describe another semicircle, *b,* with a radius of eleven inches. Cut out the semicircle strip *cdef* and join *cd* and *ef* with gummed tape, overlapping points *d* and *e* about a half inch. This forms the first part of the miter, the smaller circumference fitting the head. To form the top section (Fig. 23B, No. 2), draw a circle with a radius of seven and one-quarter inches, and another just an inch smaller.

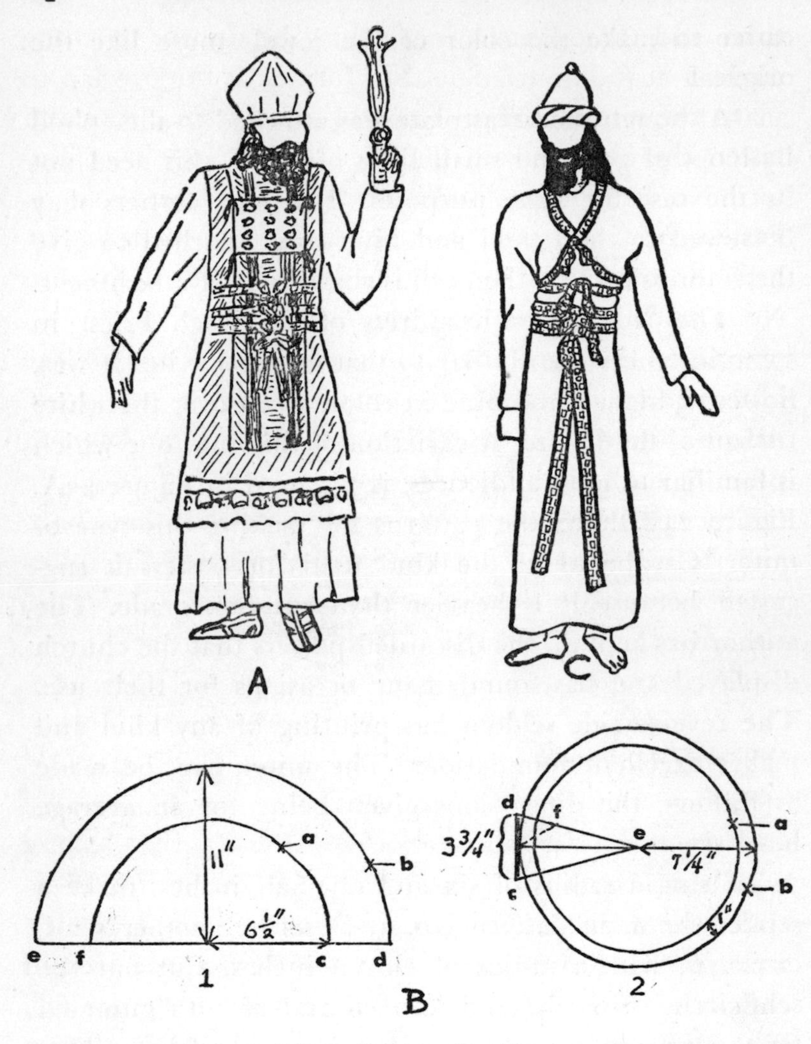

Figure 23—A: A High Priest. B: Pattern for miter. C: A Levite.

This inch constitutes the part to be fastened to the first section, making half-inch or larger slits from circle *b* to circle *a*. Extend the radii *ed* and *ec* so that a line three and three-fourths inches may be drawn, touching circle *b* at *f*. The triangle thus formed is the overlap to make the second section stand up. Cut from *c* to *e* and fasten the overlap with gummed tape. Circle *a* of pattern No. 2 should fit over circle *b* of pattern No. 1. Fasten the small tabs that you have cut on pattern No. 2 to the outside of the larger circumference of pattern No. 1 with Scotch tape or gummed tape.

Over this cardboard foundation place one of the blue cheesecloth kerchiefs of the Hebrew headdress. Around the edge of the miter that fits the head, sew a piece of dark cloth tape from ear to ear. Continue the rest of the tape around the head, over the blue cloth, and tie in the rear. The tape will help hold the miter more securely on the head. The ends of the blue material covering the foundation should fall in the rear.

The Pharisee

As a mark of distinction for the Pharisee, along with the long-sleeved tunic and wide girdle (differentiated from the Levite's narrow many-wrapped girdle), a prayer shawl or ritual garment may be wrapped around the waist similar to that of the Assyrian in Figure 6C. The Pharisee also wears a domed turban as in Figure 24A. The turban may be made as follows.

Again using cardboard from old posters, cut three pieces in the form shown in Figures 24A and 24B, the middle one, *a,* two inches higher than the side sections *b* and *c,* and having a curved edge on the bottom as

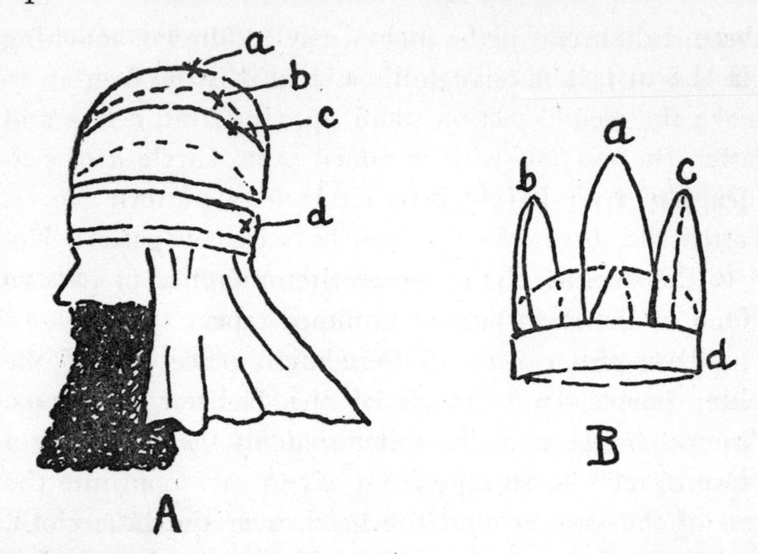

Figure 24—A: Domed turban of Pharisee. B: Pattern for turban.

well as the top. Secure these pieces to a skullcap with Mystik Tape, a tape that clings equally as well to fabric as to paper. The middle piece, *a,* should be cut to fit the head from front to rear. The two outside pieces, *b* and *c,* fit around the edge of the cap. To the edge of the cap, a two-inch band *d* of heavy cloth tape is sewed. This band should fit the head snugly. Between the three sections, *a, b* and *c,* place, very loosely, paddings of white cheesecloth so that they do not quite come to the top. Over the whole foundation drape double thicknesses of off-white cheesecloth so that the form of a tri-domed turban is maintained. The off-white material should come just to the top edge of the band around the head. As with the High Priest and Levite, long hair should be worn in the rear. Sometimes a cloth hung from the rear of the turban may be worn as in Figure 24A.

Pilate and His Wife

The toga is the prominent item of Pilate's costume. One of the short-sleeved or draped-sheet tunics should be worn under the toga. The toga itself should have a deep purple border as a mark of high office, and draped in the simple manner described under "The Cloak and Overdrape" in Section I.

For footwear, the Roman boot is appropriate. This is the heavy woolen sock dyed leather-brown with long brown or black shoestrings sewn in lacing effect from toe to top.

Pilate's wife should be dressed in the conventional Roman matron's costume. This involves the tunic and the shorter tunic. Use either a tunic draped in the Ionic manner, or the sleeveless type as shown in Figure 1A to which the long sleeves have been added. The long-sleeved tunic, rather than the draped Ionic one, probably would be more comfortable for the person portraying the wife of Pilate, since the shorter tunic should be worn also. The shorter tunic reaches the knees and should have the patagium or gold border on the hem.

As the wife of a Roman official, Pilate's wife would probably wear a coronet of gold over which the palla is thrown, either hanging straight over the shoulders or draped with the right end thrown over the left shoulder

Figure 25—Child's tunic.

and arm. If thrown over the shoulder, an ornate clasp may be used to hold the drape in place.

The Children

Children are simply clothed. A short tunic with a colorful girdle, sometimes a dark-colored skullcap, are all that are needed. Unlike the adult, a child will not cause humor should he go barefoot. If at all possible, no covering for the feet should be used. However, cold, dirty floors in the winter, along with the scanty costumes, are not appreciated by parents, so sandals may be worn and still be in keeping with the picture.

The tunic is like that of the adult except that it is knee-length and has short sleeves. An old nightgown may be shortened, the buttons removed and both edges down the front covered with a narrow band of colorful material, continuing around the neck in the manner of the tunic worn by the twelve-year-old Jesus in the picture *Christ in the Temple* by Hofman, where He is shown talking with the priests.

Figure 25 illustrates this kind of tunic. The tunic need not be white; it may be dyed tan, dark green, dark blue (not navy), or ochre-yellow.

If the child is impersonating an adult, he should be costumed as nearly like an adult as possible. In that case, the nightgown need not be shortened, but the neck camouflaged as previously indicated. If a sheet from a child's bed is available, it may be draped as for an adult.

The author is aware that not many children wear nightgowns at the present time, pajamas being more in vogue. With this in mind, an old sheet is large enough to cut and sew into tunic form.

Section Four

Anachronisms and Admonitions

Some admonitions are necessary as to what *not* to wear when impersonating Biblical characters. Church productions for many years have been such slipshod affairs that too often those participating, especially the adults, will try to do whatever seems the easiest with little thought as to the incongruity of the picture they are creating.

Men's shirts, modern trousers, shoes, wrist watches, colored nail polish, bobby pins, and spectacles have no place in a Biblical costume. Certainly no illusion of Biblical times is created with the wearing of modern apparel. Some participants are most co-operative when the incongruity is pointed out to them, others feel the production is not important enough to remove such items. With the latter, who are fortunately in the minority, the director will have to be quite firm and insist that the men remove their shirts and trousers, the women their colored nail polish. "I'll just roll up my trousers," is a common remark heard in church casts. It is better, before the production, to prevent any possibility of one trouser leg coming down during an important scene. Shirts can not be tucked in at the neck so that they will be comfortable and still not show. The actor will feel much more like Peter and *look* like Peter if he takes off these modern garments and walks the stage in clothes that have more of the true feeling of our ancients.

Bobby pins should never be worn where they show in the slightest degree. Colored nail polish is not to be tolerated. The director should have some polish remover on hand in case one of the ladies "forgets" to remove her polish at home.

Glasses should not be worn on the stage, even by those who claim they can not see without them. Glasses reflect the lights and hide the expression in the eyes that should be seen by the audience. Then, too, our Biblical people did not know what spectacles were, so they are discarded for the sake of consistency.

There have been amateur actors who literally could see nothing but light and dark or extremely vague outlines of figures without their glasses, but who handed their second pair of eyes to an assistant just before they entered the stage. Of course, they did not wait until the night of production to get along without their visual aids, but started early in the rehearsal period to go without them. They claim it was not as difficult as they first had anticipated. There was the added fact that they were able to forget themselves and feel like the characters they were creating because they were not so conscious of the many eyes watching them.

Let there be nothing to distract the eye. The costumes should blend into the picture with no discordant note. The audience will notice the least discrepancy in a production, especially in regard to that which meets the eye.

To costume a play involving many characters puts undue pressure on the costume department. The author has found more amateur groups enjoying drama presentations longer when they avoided large casts until they acquired larger wardrobes. Starting small but firmly and growing gradually has been the making of many a sturdy drama group, whether composed of children or adults. Only a very few have survived trying to make an impression with a big splurge at the start. So often failure has been the result. Of course, if the minister or principal urges the use of as many in the cast as possible, the director has a very real problem and quite often one which, as has been indicated, does not have too happy an ending.

Costuming Biblical characters can be real enjoyment for those who take pleasure in handling textiles, and who have a sincere desire to present a picture that is both pleasing and authentic in appearance. The audience will react favorably to such a picture and will gain much in the way of inspiration, and the effort expended will be a worth-while and satisfying experience.

Bibliography

Abingdon Bible Commentary. Nashville, Tennessee: Abingdon-Cokesbury Press.

BARTON, LUCY. *Historic Costume for the Stage*. Boston: Walter H. Baker Company.

EVANS, MARIA MILLINGTON. *Chapters on Greek Dress*. New York: Macmillan Company.

GRIMBALL, ELIZABETH B. AND WELLS, RHEA. *Costuming a Play*. New York: The Century Company.

HOUSTON, MARY G. *Ancient Greek, Roman and Byzantine Costume and Decoration*. London: A. & C. Black, Ltd.

HOUSTON, MARY G. AND HORNBLOWER, FLORENCE S. *Ancient Egyptian, Assyrian and Persian Costumes*. London: A. & C. Black, Ltd.

KÖHLER, CARL. *A History of Costume*. London: George G. Harrap & Company.

LEEMING, JOSEPH. *The Costume Book for Parties and Plays*. New York: Frederick A. Stokes Company.

LESTER, KATHERINE MORRIS. *Historic Costume*. Peoria, Illinois: The Manual Arts Press.

WRIGHT, MARION LOGAN. *Biblical Costume*. London: Society for Promoting Christian Knowledge.

References

Historical Background

Abingdon Bible Commentary
Chapters on Greek Dress—Evans
Historic Costume—Lester
Historic Costume for the Stage—Barton
History of Costume, A—Köhler

Designs and Decorations

Ancient Egyptian, Assyrian and Persian Costumes—Houston and Hornblower
Ancient Greek, Roman and Byzantine Costume and Decoration—Houston
Historic Costume for the Stage—Barton

Illustrations

Biblical Costume—Wright
Chapters on Greek Dress—Evans
Costume Book for Parties and Plays (Greek and Roman)—Leeming
Costuming a Play (Egyptian, Greek, Roman, Assyrian)—Grimball and Wells
Historic Costume for the Stage—Barton
History of Costume, A—Köhler

Accessories

Historic Costume for the Stage—Barton

General

Biblical Costume—Wright
Historic Costume—Lester
Historic Costume for the Stage—Barton

Index